THE SIMPLICITY OF LIFE

Written by
Cisco Fernandes

Copyright © 2008 by Cisco Fernandes

All rights reserved.

Printed in the United States of America

Published by Lulu.com

ISBN 978-1-4357-1524-0

for Joe...

5 STAGES

1. Denial
2. Anger
3. Fear
4. Bargaining
5. Acceptance

BREADCRUMBS

I believe that clichés are like breadcrumbs left behind by the wise who have found their way through life's dense forest. Instinctively they strike a cord inside us. Maybe it's one that we've heard many times before but never listened to because it didn't apply to us in our present day lives. It's not until a specific event that crosses our path in life, or we reach a moment in our lives that a certain cliché touches us that it feels as though it's speaking directly to us. They inspire us in moments of need; comfort us in times of sorrow. They are as numerous as there are stars in the night sky. There seems to be just one problem with these eloquent clues to life. Just as the night stars, clichés are so numerous that we may have a tendency to take them for granted. They become overused and their significance is viewed as unoriginal and predictable. That wonderful, connected feeling that we first felt may tend to wane after awhile, you hear them used so often, over used honestly at times. Their importance may even go entirely unheard simply because it is what it is: a cliché.

Our ego may even convince us, after some time that we were silly for feeling that way in the first place. It's the certain individual that upon finding this breadcrumb picks it up, puts it in their pocket where it becomes interwoven into the very fabric of their being. In fact it's this person that understands its significance and sets out to find more, not satisfied with simply just stumbling across one from time to time as they trek through this dense forest of life. With understanding comes meaning; with meaning comes purpose and direction; the same direction that those wiser than us have walked and have been kind enough to unselfishly leave behind a breadcrumb.

CONTENTS

1   Me

2   The Accident

3   Rehab and Beyond

4   Hand Envy

5   Driver and Passenger

6   The Bed

7   Jenn

8   The Great Garbage Debate

9   Epilogue

Chapter One

ME

I guess one of my earliest memories of challenge was when I was about nine and new to Hayestown Avenue Elementary School in Danbury, Connecticut, the third grade. I didn't know anyone. I was very shy and very short but was a very fast runner and it was Field Day; my day to show everyone in the school how cool the new kid was. If there was one thing I was confident about myself, it was this: I was one quick little bastard! The event was a race around the entire school yard, about a quarter mile. I scanned the other kids trying to find my competition, the gym teacher blew his whistle and I was off. I ran so fast I didn't think about pacing myself or anything I just ran as fast as I could. "Don't look back, just go, go, go, and show them all." I was out in front and feeling fantastic and absolutely free as I rounded the first and second corners of the yard. Then I hit corner three and the home stretch was straight ahead. This is when it all hit me, my heart was beating out of my chest and I could hardly breathe, my legs felt like lead. I looked out to my right and caught sight of Eddie. "Damn it, he caught up" and I was running out of gas real fast. "I can't believe I'm going to lose." I remember digging down as deep as I could to find the strength to keep going, "don't stop, not now." I couldn't, I was so tired, "I can't go anymore" I was so tired, I started to pull up and slow down. I was so sure Eddie would be passing me any moment now, but he didn't "what happened?" I looked over, then back and Eddie had run out of steam too. I remember this story, this one moment in my life because of what happened next. I became totally filled with renewed energy, as if from nowhere, "I'm going to win, HOLY SHIT, I'm going to win!" I ran as fast as I could to the finish line, never looking back and I won! The short skinny new kid won the big race. God I thought I was king of the world that day. This memory always stood with me, it was one I leaned on a lot through the years as life showed me her adverse ways.

Let's see where to start? I'll try and keep this as short, simple and undramatic as I possibly can. My mother started studying to become a Jehovah's Witness literally while she was in the hospital after just giving birth to me, the youngest of four children. She 'almost died giving birth to me' as she would constantly remind me in the future, and that's when the neighbors, who were Jehovah's Witness', visited her and of course left reading material, which then lead to my enslavement. My mother is a complex person to say the least. After having her fourth child from a third man, she found god, and dedicated her entire life to her cult.....I mean religion. She gave new meaning to the word 'STRICT'. My big brother Joe (being two and a half year older than me) and myself used to draw her wrath most of the time, getting our daily beatings. I'm not talking like: the bent over the knee, a couple of swats and the "don't ever do that again" spanking. Ours was a beating, no exaggerating, seriously. It always started with the phrase: "You're gonna get the beating of your life". The routine was to go to our room, pull down our pants and kneel over our bed and get spanked with a cut off piece of garden hose as she screams at us, until my mother was tired. My brother always went first, the anticipation of me being next never got old.

Not really being a social child in elementary school and not being allowed to interact with anyone who wasn't in the religion, I didn't realize that this type of punishment wasn't normal. It wasn't until I reached middle school that my eyes began to open. My father had left us in the middle of the night. He worked all of the time and was never around; never really the 'fatherly type' and his leaving didn't help with the beatings much. It kinda seemed odd to me that such a god fearing woman could beat us with such anger, and I really didn't think that we were that bad, but I was a child and she was my mother. We had to leave our home, the home that I lived in since I was that little boy on that special Field Day, and move to the local projects. Going to Rodgers Park Middle School certainly opened my eyes a lot. Living in the Mill Ridge projects, the school bus ride to school was always chaotic, everyone was loud and an occasional fight would brake out. Living in government subsidized housing there was a wide array of ethnicity: black, brown and white. Myself coming from Portuguese and Puerto Rican descant I fell into the 'brown' crowd, except I didn't and was prejudged against by all, being an easy target. I was still short, skinny and withdrawn. I didn't fall into any crowd; I was mostly in shock the first year. This school had its own police officer patrolling the grounds, and you can still count on a daily lunch room brawl. It felt kinda like middle school prison, kids jumping up on the large lunch room tables screaming "FIGHT, FIGHT, FIGHT"! It was crazy. I was around thirteen, and was lost and so I was left back in the seventh grade, I was so embarrassed. As an adult now and looking back it's really no wonder why I failed, considering what was going on in my life at the time, never any family communication, never really knowing what's going on. My dad had legally divorced my mom and that's all we heard that year. Again, I could never understand why she literally talked about him every day, always in a negative way. I swear I think that was it for her, she never spoke of men again in a positive way. She never dated, never even hinted at interest in any man, and we were in a cult for god's sake full of eligible single men encouraged to date within the community. If anything her animosity towards men intensified and me and Joe drew her wrath even more. To finish my point, failing the seventh grade was a blessing in disguise, I became a bad boy and puberty kicked in and I really discovered girls, I was aware of them before but this was a whole different awareness. I also belonged to a fraternity, the 'left back club'. My second year of seventh grade was a turning point in my childhood development. I started selling blow pops to earn money so I can buy the latest Nike sneakers, I knew I'd never get my mom to buy me them. I learned of rock music from my friends, I'll never forget hearing Crazy Train by Ozzy Osbourne for the first time. I read The Hobbit by J.R.R. Tolkien which opened my eyes; I had never been exposed to the outside "WORLD" as Jehovah's Witness' refer to. Anything, any written word, thought or belief that didn't originate from themselves is considered "WORLDLY" or not of their world, and is forbidden. I now saw life differently and began to develop relationships in secret, outside the organization, the double life had begun and once again my life was about to take a hard left turn.

My brother Joe had already turned sixteen and all he wanted, like any other red blooded American boy his age wants, is his drivers license. My mother saw it as his ticket to freedom and refused to allow him to get it. They fought over it for weeks and he told me he was so sick of her and I agreed, I think we were approaching that age that my mother felt that she was losing her grip on us. Joe and I were still as close as ever and we started plotting a scheme to get out of this situation, Joe really wanted his license. Then one day we got out of school early and were hanging out, it was more like I was tagging along and hanging out with my brother's friends. It was getting late and I started getting that panicky feeling because I knew my mother would be home soon from her bible studies and would be expecting us home soon after. I also knew what would happen if we were late, and god forbid if she didn't believe us, which she didn't half of the time. I remember telling Joe 'that we had to go home' but he was busy riding some kids' dirt bike around the neighborhood, he told me to go ahead and he'd catch up. He never did and our childhood bond was broken forever. He called the house later, which felt like an eternity under my mother's interrogation as to my brother's whereabouts. She was freaking out on the phone with him and finished with: "WHEN YOU GET HOME YOUR GONNA GET THE BEATING OF YOUR LIFE"! Well Joe never did get that beating because he never came home, and I don't blame him one bit. At the time I did though, but I was just a kid who lost his big brother and my world just got rocked.

    For the next couple of weeks I barely came out of my room other than to go to The Kingdom Hall for worship and we only did that three times a week, two hours each meeting. I had packed a book bag full of clothes and things that I would bring with me when Joe would come back for me. I waited and waited driving myself mad and so I taught myself how to juggle, not sure why juggling, but it was something I could do alone and it helped keep my hands busy. Idle hands you know. Joe never did come for me; I later came to understand that he was living with my father who I still hadn't seen since he left. My whole life, my whole identity was lost, whatever Joe liked I liked, whatever he thought was cool I thought the same. I remember that this was the beginning of what I call my 'chameleon years' where I took bits and pieces of personality from my peers that I liked and applied them to myself, trying to find myself. For the next two years I engulfed myself into the religion I was born into. It taught me much. It taught me self discipline, confidence in public speaking (once a month I had to give a five minute speech in front of the whole congregation of two hundred) it was always such a rush every time I stepped up on stage, I could've stood up there all night. I always aced the 'in front of the class' reports in school. It also taught me the teaching of Jesus Christ's love for man. I must've read the bible from cover to cover ten to fifteen times alone. As well as learning to debate against other religions beliefs, dogmas verses dogmas, how ironic.

Now here I am the soul survivor of a family of six, and now it's just me and my mother. Without going into gory detail, I'll briefly detail the chain of events that led to this. First, when I was in second grade we had moved from Connecticut to California, driving across the country in a Ford Galaxy sedan, four kids (I always got stuck in the middle) and towing a trailer, which we lived in. I must admit it was a great memory, because we stopped off at just about every state along the way and took in the sites. Seeing Niagara Falls, the Grand Canyon and driving through the Mojave Desert are memories I'll keep with me always. When we arrived in California that's when all hell broke loose, living in a trailer at a campground wasn't the ideal situation. We only lasted a year and a half when it was decided that we were moving back home, that's when I lost my oldest brother John. The story goes: John had made some friends and didn't want to leave. What did I know, I was only eight years old and I only got second hand information. John had gotten into a huge fight with my father. He had come home to our trailer and what happened next I swear I saw first hand: John (was eighteen, tall and lanky) walked in and my mother hauled off and slapped him across his face and insisted that he was leaving with us. John, to our astonishment, grabbed my mother's arms and pushed her back, no one had ever resisted my mother's wrath, but he did that one final time. My mother, being all of what 4'11" and ninety pounds, of course fell back and hit her head and started screaming 'bloody murder'. She insisted on going to the emergency room to get it checked out, we all went with her except John who just left and that's the last time I saw him. The drive back felt a little weird without one brother, but there was more room, I even got a window to myself (honestly I had never had much of a relationship with him, maybe the age difference) and I shared the whole back seat with my best friend Joe.

    After getting situated again in Connecticut my father was the next domino to fall, he left without saying a word. I remember it was late at night. Me and Joe were already in our bedroom and mom and dad were having a fight as usual. I heard the front door slam so I ran to my bedroom window and saw my dad with a handful of clothes still on their hangers. I watched as he threw them into the backseat then he got into the car and drove away. I was very confused and didn't know if my mother would leave too. My father never came home again.

To say the least my mother wasn't adjusting well with this new situation. Now don't get me wrong, I have love for both of my parents, I just don't respect them and the decisions that they've made. I know they 'tried', but there's a difference between trying and doing, only age would show me this lesson, that and my parents poor example. My mother had a meltdown and she couldn't work anymore, her anxiety or something, and we went on welfare which of course led to our moving to the projects. My sister Angela was the next, she fell in love with one of the boys in the neighborhood which was a sin to my mother, he didn't belong to the congregation, and he was a "WORLDLY BOY". My sister of course chose her heart and she left, which just left me and Joe alone with my mother and her bitterness. I just explained how I lost my big brother Joe, so it was just me and my mother. After Joe left the beatings stopped. I think she was scared I was next to go.

That's the backwards chronological order of how the dominoes fell in my family and I was the last. After throwing myself into my ministries I decided to get baptized, much to my mother's pleasure. I was the first child in the family to get baptized, I guess now I really needed something to believe in. Everything seemed fine for the next two years, as long as I was doing everything that my mother approved of. High school changed everything. I remember having this teacher in social studies who I thought was really cool and made learning fun. We were learning about Tibetan Buddhist monks and their lifestyle of peace and enlightenment through discipline. Now as a

Jehovah's Witness your belief system is that 'yours' is the only true religion and all others will be destroyed at Armageddon (belief system based on fear). I remember feeling that this can't be right. How can God kill these people who have practiced their beliefs in peace for thousands of years, Buddhism started 500 years before Christ was born, just because they didn't belong to this religion that has just begun over a hundred years ago? I brought this discussion up with the elders in the congregation and the best they could come up with is: 'if they deserve, then Jehovah will bring them to his flock'. I was horrified. It was roughly about this same time that the head elder's daughter, Rebecca, after months of secrecy, decided to go public and profess her love to her first cousin Brian (who I was good friends with, him and his younger brother Kyle) and their plans to marry. I was crushed, I had no idea and was torn because I loved Brian as my surrogate older brother but didn't agree with this decision. It also created a rift in the congregation, boy the gossip ran rampant, all behind closed doors. Would the Tibetan monks have behaved the same way? I really started to see hypocrisy everywhere and my respect for such prestigious archetype figures started to falter. I started to separate myself from those in the religion, I guess I stopped caring and I'm sure my mother could sense this because she started in with the guilt trips. 'You better never leave me; I don't want to take a family portrait all alone'. I was a junior in high school and started dating this girl Kristen, who we used to flirt and 'in school' date when we were in junior high (I could never see her outside of school, my mother would have killed me). She always held a special place in my heart; she was my first love and one of the rare persons that I kept in contact with over the years. The double life reemerged again, and this time I wasn't afraid of my mother. I was torn though; I felt trapped was a more accurate definition of my mental state. I didn't want to leave my mother alone, but I knew I couldn't live this life that my mother had planned out for me. What do I do, how can I live this lie of a life? I felt so guilty, but I didn't want anything outrageous I just wanted to live my life, mine not anyone else's. I just wanted to live a normal life (something that still resonates with me even today).

After graduation (my father didn't even attend that, and again I was the first in my family to graduate high school) I knew something had to give. I was rebelling properly, drinking and smoking on a regular basis with the guys from work, forget about the ladies that I met who weren't god fearing. I convinced myself that if I'm honest enough with my mother, communicate with her that I'm going to move out and that our relationship doesn't have to end, I just needed my INDEPENDENCE. Of course it didn't go that well and my mother disowned me. It took months before she even took my phone calls. To her I disowned her by living my life, not the one she planned for me. After some months of struggling on my own I knew I needed help and refused to move back home so I sought out my father, figuring he at least owed me one. To my surprise he welcomed me to his house to live for a while. We talked a lot, usually while drinking the night away. I learned that he regretted a lot of the decisions that he'd made over the years but he felt it was too late to do anything. I swore I would never live my life with regret.

I reunited with my brother Joe after he got out of the Marines, but we were both different people now. Life had taken us on different paths, molded us into different people and although we both loved each other, that incredible close bond was forever broken. I guess I was still that little brother who longed for that closeness to return. It was also because of my brother that I met Jenn, my best friend and eventual wife. They worked together and he hooked me up with a job at the same place. Jenn was an artist and didn't care much for what society thought of her. She also had her own set of rules in life, never took no for an answer and the word "can't" was not in her vocabulary. She's the only person I know that when she wanted to do something she just did it, almost not knowing that failure existed. Her spirit shined and her confidence drew people into her world. I'll forever be in debt to him for helping me find her, as she would save me on more than one occasion in my life. As the years go on in my life, she has taught me a great deal, more than I could have ever possibly imagined. I believe (to me personally) that life itself is a constant process of learning; we learn and grow until we die. Jenn taught me how to 'break the cycle' which really is a life long exercise. Life's experiences, whether they were adverse or easy are just that, experiences to reflect back on for future decision making. There are no such things as absolutes and to be cautiously optimistic about every one and everything.

ME

Like the little boy who won that race that fateful summer afternoon, I learned no matter how tired I am, whether mentally or physically, to never ever give up or give in. I have a special reserve, another gear. In growing up and then growing out I really began to believe that maybe I really am someone special, it just felt right and I was finding my way. It would only take a tragedy, true love and courage I never knew I had, to truly believe. I never knew how simple life really is.

I am Francisco Luis Fernandes, I am someone special. No really, I am!

THE SIMPLICITY OF LIFE

Chapter Two

THE ACCIDENT

The date was June 17, 2000. I was 29, 3 months away from my 30th birthday. I was mentally preparing myself, (convincing myself), that the 30`s were the decade of life where you establish yourself as an adult. My personal identity had finally begun to establish itself. I for the most part, knew who I was, shed a lot of my adolescent insecurities and for the first time since "high school" my drinking and partying days had peaked and I was sober. I found myself wanting to be a father, so I married my best friend after we had worked out all of our youthful trivial issues. I set myself up for a child by getting a job that he or she would be proud of, something besides bartending, and bought a car. I had my Mustang, not a real family car, but man did I love it. Living in Brooklyn, our apartment was huge, over two thousand square feet, which we completely renovated ourselves, Jenn's idea, with help from our friend Tod (it was a butchers shop before, now completely gutted) cathedral ceilings, we even had a little back yard. It was beautiful. Our living situation was all set. My days of bartending in the West Village in Manhattan were behind me. I worked out all of my youthful craziness and I finally felt like I was focused. Bartending in New York in itself is like a drug. I loved it. It had everything I could have ever wanted in a job, except no one ever warned me. The catch was that I had to sell my soul for a job that rewarded hard work, vampire hours (8p.m. till 5a.m.) and incredible pay, along with all the booze, drugs and attention from other women that any man could ever ask for. Behind the bar is like being on stage. Everyone begging for your attention and on a Friday or Saturday night you got 3 to 4 people deep for hours. For me the more chaotic a night, the better the night was. Music screaming, people fighting, corny guys hitting on the pretty girls, everyone buying you shots and offering you everything and anything you could ever possibly imagine, the bouncer throws another out, adrenaline in overdrive, what a rush. Regulars yell out your name as they enter, egos now inflated, and everyone loves your drinks, including the shot you created earlier that night. In the past, I had read about an individuals ego from the perspective of Freud and Jung, and other philosophies from the far east and India, I tried to understand it's role in my life and I was still at it's mercy once I stepped behind the bar. That's where the "selling" comes in, you see myself and Jenn had been together for 8 years, we grew up together, lived in 3 different states together, lived together,

THE ACCIDENT

lived apart and at one time we lived in the east village in Manhattan while going to the same college and even worked at the school store together. We were together twenty four hours a day. People thought we were crazy. We were just literally best friends and lovers. We did it all before we were 30. You see, no matter what our situation seemed to be, it was understood that any problems that we encountered we would work it out somehow, somewhere, whatever it takes, however long it took. I should have known better.

What happened next is what I liken to a mix drink of the mind: 1) Add one part insecurity: a new husband 'title', I was freaking out that I was really married even though we had lived together for 8 years already. 2) One part animosity: from previous unresolved issues that I had felt slighted. 3) Mix in a ridiculous amount of 'a need for attention' from other girls. What you wind up with is something called **_amnesia_**. I forgot it was "us", not Cisco and Jenn and I knew that I needed time to reflect (or so I convinced myself). What I needed to do was talk, instead, I took her for granted.

I suppose, like most people, I've always felt different from my peers, special in a way, but I was wasting time away, expelling all of my demons through alcohol and drugs, afraid to become the person I felt destined to be. But now was different. The sun began to shine again. Trusting myself and my instincts, I found a new job, one that's fulfilling, with a group of artist in Brooklyn named Art Asylum, making action figures. It felt more like a family then a job. God I felt like a little kid getting paid to play, since I was such a comic book and action figure geek. Me and Jenn finally 'talked' and my marriage to my best friend was finally beginning to feel normal. It seems so ridiculous now, but at the time I felt as though I had to behave like someone else, like a 'Married Man', whatever that's supposed to be. We had only been married just under a year but I finally got over it, I got it. Just be me! Don't be afraid, just stop, relax, open your eyes and listen to your inner voice whispering. Everything felt aligned.

For our one year anniversary I made reservations to rent a cabin at a campground to surprise Jenn. Those were the two things we loved to do, build sandcastles on the beach and go camping in upstate New York. We had so much fun that weekend. I brought my skateboard and Jenn brought her roller skates. The first night we celebrated by eating some wedding cake that we froze on our wedding day and the next morning I dropped Jenn off at the kids crafts class while I went to play basketball. Later that night, it stormed so hard that there were mudslides and we ran to the arcade through the pouring rain. We played video games for hours as the thunder and lighting roared. The next morning we went for a skate and I remember carrying her over a huge puddle as an onlooker remarked how cute we looked. It was a perfect weekend and we felt so connected. We planned another trip at a closer location the next month. This one had horseback riding and skydiving. We showed up early and were so excited. We went horse back riding first. It was my first time and I loved it

THE ACCIDENT

but I don't think Jenn shared the same enthusiasm as I did. I remember saying aloud, "I hope I don't do a Christopher Reeve!" as I was riding my horse Winston. It's funny in retrospect; it was almost as if I was tempting fate, something I'd done a million times before. I also realize now, that when you don't know a person that has a spinal cord injury or is afflicted with a physical disability, you might think it sounds funny to say such a flip comment.

After working up a ferocious appetite, and pigging out back at the camp, we took a nap. I can still remember that nap as if it were yesterday, holding Jenn in one arm until it went numb, smelling the campfire in her hair, we slept solid for a couple of hours. It felt so right. It would be the last time I held her like that, at least for a long while. Jenn wanted to go swimming before it got late so we went up to the pool. I was just going to lounge poolside and read a book and watch her play around in the water like the child at heart that she is. Jenn sat at the edge of the pool, toes dangling in the water, she says: "if you go in I'll go in", so I said "sure". As much as we are alike, we are so different. Jenn is a toe tipper, feeling the temperature of the water, gradually adjusting to it and then slowly wades in. Me, I just go for it, get it over with, like a band aid, one quick motion, dive in head first. I'll adjust to the water later. I've always been that way. Always have been, always will be. I like that about me, and even now, I would never change that about myself. So that's what I did, walked to the deep end of the pool, not realizing it was only 4 feet deep. It looked like a regulation size pool and even though I didn't see any "NO DIVING" signs anywhere, I ultimately am responsible for myself; I mean there were other people in the pool, matter of fact there were quite a few. I grew up around pools and always took pride in my diving skills: get good air, nice arc, keep your head tucked between your out stretched arms, fingers pointed straight ahead and most important, point those toes and splash as little as possible. So here I go, good air and another perfect dive. Jenn will be impressed, even though she will never admit it. 'Bam!'... "Holy Shit I hit my head". It didn't seem so bad at the moment; I just knew I had to get to the surface to check for blood. It was at this moment that I realized I couldn't move a muscle in my body. I was face down, eyes wide open, chlorine stinging my eyes and I started freaking out. "I CAN'T MOVE, SOMEBODY HELP!!!." Muffled sounds all around me, everything was so chaotic, I couldn't do anything. I was frantic. I thought: "I'm gonna die, this is it, I'm gonna die!" This wasn't one of those close calls you get when you think: "WOW, that was close, I could've died." I always felt like I was going to die a young man but I wasn't ready yet. Oh God not now, not like this. I remember seeing a hand in front of me. I figured it was somebody standing right next to me unaware that I was right there below him dying, he was so oblivious. I remember being close enough to him but I just couldn't touch him so I did the next best thing. I bit his hand. My fight/flight response. Little did I realize that it was my own hand that I had bit. It turned out to be a blessing in disguise. Somehow as I bit my hand it turned my head to the side and it caused my head to surface. Not enough to breath air but enough to see my angel starring at me. I saw Jenn, still poolside just

THE ACCIDENT

looking at me, thinking I was playing "dead man's float" and waiting for her to rescue me. It was a test of wills to see who would give in first. Jenn usually won. Now, in hindsight, I realize how stupid of a game that really is and we used to play it all of the time. I saw her looking at me and suddenly my panic, my frantic fear of drowning, just stopped. A moment of clarity overtook me. I just thought, "Jenn`s gonna see me die, right in front of her eyes. Hold on Damn it, just Hold On!" Everything seemingly just slowed down and I screamed out to her with my right eye, "Come get me!" I screamed as loud as I could with my eye and she did. It seemed like everything was in slow motion. She waded slowly towards me, as if an angel descended down from the heavens to save me. Jenn lifted my head so gently out of the water and I took in the longest, loudest, ugliest gasp of air (nothing like the movies) and all I could say was: "Thank you, Thank you!" She knew something wasn't right. I was yelling, "Something's wrong, something's wrong!" Jenn kept telling me to calm down because people all around us began looking. She didn't realize the severity of the situation.

You see, before that fateful day, Jenn was used to me and my crazy ways, like bungee jumping with a concussion, (although I didn't know I had a concussion at the time), skateboarding with a sprained ankle or climbing a statue in Washington Square Park and falling off. I never once broke a bone, plenty of hair line fractures, sprains and other physical mishaps. People used to say 'you should be careful' whenever I talked about not breaking a bone. Guess I saved it all up for this fateful day.

Jenn didn't understand what was happening, until she saw my bloody hand. I told her that I couldn't move and from that moment on she just took over. She rolled me onto my back and slowly pulled me to the shallow end, talking to me the whole time. It was at this time that some 'Good Samaritan' realizing the situation, grabbed my feet and helped Jenn. I sure wish I got his name to thank him for his brave, unselfish act. I then remember feeling incredibly tired (it's remarkable how the human body reacts to trauma, trying to alleviate the stress) and all I wanted to do was to close my eyes and take a quick nap. Jenn saw this and immediately started yelling at me to look at her, stay awake and to keep looking at her. There's so much confusion going on, I hear noises that I can't understand. I just want everything to stop, and my eyelids feel soooo heavy, it took every bit of strength to keep them open. Sounds crazy that it took that amount of energy to keep my eyes open but it certainly felt so. I had to, Jenn kept yelling at me. She tells me days later that she instinctively felt that if I closed my eyes that I would've never woken up, she was probably right. That's number 2 on the "Saving Cisco's life" continuum. I'm so grateful to her for keeping me awake, for not only the obvious, but I'm so glad that I remember everything. I never want to forget what happened to me, not one moment.

After what felt like an eternity, I finally get loaded into the ambulance and it's during the ride that I really knew something was seriously wrong with me by the looks on the faces of the 2 female paramedics. I have no idea what they were doing but they were moving all

THE ACCIDENT

around me in a hectic manner checking my vital signs, I guess, and putting a neck brace on very carefully. They too kept telling me to keep my eyes open. It was around then that I knew our camping trip was over. As unbelievable as this sounds; what happens next really did happen, although at the time I had no idea what was going on. You see the state ambulance was taking too long, so the local ambulance took me and on the way to the hospital the two crossed paths on some bridge, they stopped traffic, and for some crazy reason transferred me from one ambulance to the other. I can only imagine what this scene looked like from the perspective of those that got caught in this traffic jam. I now noticed that my entire body was shaking uncontrollably. Did it just begin or was it doing it before and now I just realized it? It was such an outer body experience. I remember being strapped to a wooden board to stabilize my body which seemed to amplify the vibrations and my teeth were chattering. Suddenly, I'm in the hospital, voices all around me but no one is talking to me, more confusion, chaos even, I don't understand. I'm freezing right down to my very core. I've never felt so cold. I finally get out of my mouth, "can I please have a blanket?" then was told 'no' because I had a fever, "WHAT THE HELL ARE YOU TALKING ABOUT!" and then I hear them putting ice packs in my crotch and underarms. Suddenly a voice says, "You might feel some discomfort for a moment." The feeling of screws being drilled into my scull is what that 'discomfort' was. I don't remember much after that.

I woke up to silence and darkness. Most of the lights had been turned off and I was still shaking but I finally had my blanket. I try looking around but couldn't even turn my head from side to side and then I hear Jenn's voice and for the first time in a long time I feel comfort. My poor girl was still in her bathing suit and she had been crying. I ask her if there was something on my head because my head felt heavy. She half laughingly responds, "Uh Yeah." The doctors had secured my head with a metal halo with a weighted bag to prevent any movement. She tells me of her conversation with the doctor. She was so brave. She tells me that I broke my neck at the C5, C6 vertebrae, completely shattering C5, so they will be removing it all together, and they will secure my neck with a titanium plate from C4 to C6, all of this being a foreign language to me at the time. Now my anatomy is a second language to me. The doctors tells her that I'm paralyzed (which was already understood), that I was a quadriplegic, that I had no movement in my hands and that I would be paralyzed from the middle of my chest down and her only response was, "But he's going to live?". At the most traumatic moment in both of our lives, my paralysis didn't matter, just whether I was going to live or die. After our talk we cried. We knew life would never be the same.

Later that night, I was moved to a room and Jenn made the dreaded phone calls. The nurse tells her to tell my father to come there tonight, which he does and when I see him and my step mother, they start crying. I can only imagine what I must have looked like. I don't remember them leaving. I fell asleep. Of what I remember for the rest of that night was waking up, what felt like every 15 minutes, in a panic attack. I later came to understand that I was not alone in this. In moments of trauma the sensation of falling asleep is a scary feeling. I would jump awake and call for Jenn who tried to sleep on the chair next to me. God, I don't know how many times I called her that first night. I wouldn't even ask her for anything. Just hearing her voice and knowing that she was there and that I was not alone was the only thing that would calm me. Jenn never complained. She never left my side, only to go back to the camp to get our things, never showed her fear and she never treated me with pity. She never even let on as to how I looked. I hadn't looked in a mirror since my accident, not sure whether that was a conscience decision or not and Jenn surely didn't volunteer one to me. I remember that she kept trying to take a picture of me, her way of capturing each moment as it happens, but to me I needed no picture to remember this moment. She's crazy like that. The doctor who performed the surgery was named Dr. Goran, a genuine man with deep blue eyes. Me and Jenn joked around and named him Dr. Goranimal. Only Jenn could help alleviate a situation with wordplay. God I don't know who I would've become without her and her support. Not to sound corny, it's just the truth.

The following couple of days become a parade of friends and family members that come to show their love and support. Again, that's when I realized that I must look a mess. My poor niece and nephew on Jennifer's side, Stephanie (13 at the time) and Josh (10 at the time) were absolutely horrified when they came to see me at the hospital. They didn't even want to come up to the bed to see me. You got to love the honesty of kids. Mostly everyone tries to be strong for your sake and put on that front, 'You look great' bullshit. You see, I'm the youngest in my 'blood' family and I never had a younger brother or sister, so I relished in being an uncle. Along with my other nephew Johnny we always seemed to do something fun, whether it was going to a Yankees game, working on some art project that Jenn had put us up to or playing wiffle ball during the holidays. We always had a blast. For someone who never had much of a family, being an uncle was more of a privilege, besides the kids were great, always appreciative of me and never shy of showing their love. So it was no surprise to see them react the way they did and I didn't blame them. I am their favorite uncle..... just kidding, (not really).

Your family and friends come 'baring gifts' so what happens is that you wind up with a shrine of yourself, cards, pictures and memorials that remind them of you as well as things that they know you like. Me being a huge New York Yankees fan as well as most of my family, so I had a semi-Yankees shrine. I was so proud. In a kind of sick way it's almost like being alive at your own funeral, at least that's how I felt. It was such an outer body experience, at least the first 19 days, being at St. Francis hospital in Poughkeepsie, New York. At this point I was on a feeding tube, I'm still not quite sure why I was put on one in the first place but at that point I wasn't questioning anything. I luckily wasn't on a trach to assist my breathing and I was just grateful for that. In fact I had tubes protruding every orifice of my body and that's when I realized that I had sensation below the chest, 'nipples down' the guys from rehab at Mount Sinai used to call it. In spinal cord injuries, doctors and therapist test your level of sensation on what's called an "Asia Scale" and I was an Asia B meaning I had sensation, even though it wasn't 100% I was grateful for what I had. Funny guys, I learned a lot from them but that's getting ahead of myself.

I guess that's why I feel so strongly about the 'simplicity of life' because in the blink of the eye, me....ME, couldn't use the bathroom by myself, dress myself, couldn't even scratch my head if I had an itch(now I know how a dog feels). When Jenn scratches my head, I could have her do it all day it feels that good. My independence had been robbed from me. The job, car and appearance issues that dominate an individual's occupation of life are suddenly pushed aside and substituted for simple ordinary 'pleasures'. I can only say this with hindsight, that 20/20 thing. The funny thing is that I felt that way, to a certain degree, already. I had read enough to understand that the essence of life is not the pursuit of material possessions or the pursuit of substance-less attention from others. Don't complain, go after your goals, don't take NO for an answer, be patient and grow. Most of life is cerebral. It's really simple and for the first time in my life I felt as though I was right there.

After a few days, I was allowed to finally eat and I couldn't believe how much I missed eating. McDonald's was my sinful choice of first 'real' food and my father went to get it. He got lost coming back and by the time he got back to the hospital my double cheeseburger and fries were cold. Not to complain but it was not the ideal first meal I was looking forward to. My appetite slowly returned and I remember thinking how on earth am I ever going to feed myself without the use of my hands. Thank God for Jenn. I wouldn't consider myself a 'germafob', but I am a clean freak. Guess that fits into that O.C.D. behavior I exhibited as a child, before doctors diagnosed this behavior and prescribe a boat full of meds. I remember as a kid telling myself that I didn't need to check the door three, four or five times. "I locked the bathroom door, it's O.K. I don't need to check it." Guess it's just discipline. That's one of the few things that I've been appreciative of and that I've taken with me to my adulthood. Growing up a Jehovah's Witness is self discipline and tons of it but again that is a topic for another chapter. Getting back to my semi 'germafob' behavior, I've always been the type of person who doesn't like anyone to touch his food, 'don't touch my slice of pizza,' no salad or food bars, no eating off of my plate or vice versa, no offense. Only Jenn, who ironically tends to be messy, (which I attest to her being an artist), seems to always have two different socks on or has no problem eating a sandwich with her hands full of paint. I on the other hand washed mine anywhere from 15 to 20 times a day. She was the only person who I felt comfortable feeding me, only her, but I still kept my eyes on her hands making sure they were clean and they were. She knows me so well. It became another bonding experience, mealtime. Jenn would jump into my bed to feed me, much to the horror of family and friends, even the nursing staff didn't say a word, mostly they'd laugh. That's another thing; she never treated me as if I were fragile even though I was broken. There was this one time she jumped into my bed to make a phone call and put the entire phone on my stomach, and started dialing, I had to finally say something before she realized what she had done, then she giggles and apologizes. Mealtime quickly becomes the only time of the day that I truly look forward to. A few days later my halo came off and was replaced with a huge plastic neck brace.

Having never been bedridden for a length of time before, I didn't know of blood pressure and it's affect on the body. I had been laying flat for days and had only recently been inclined in my bed so I can eat. Written on an erase board near my bed were the words: physical therapy 2 o'clock. The time couldn't come soon enough. I watched the clock which of course didn't help. The time finally came and in walked this therapist who looked younger than me and 60 pounds lighter than me. She was pretty and had an innocent, soft look to her face. The first session started off slowly, sit up in a fully upright position and monitor my blood pressure so I don't pass out. Great no problem, I'm thinking 'that's it, lets keep going', and so we do. The next step is to transfer me to a wheelchair and see how long I can tolerate it. A CHALLENGE. Unfortunately there wasn't another therapist or an aide around. It was my experience that there was never a nurse's aide around when you need one and nurses DIDN'T transfer patients. Anyway, my therapist was excited and thought between herself and my father that they could lift me to a wheelchair. The concept was great, the execution wasn't as much. Lifting me was no problem, the moment my butt hit the chair my body straightened right out, stiff as a board before they were able to put a seatbelt on me. I immediately shit my pants then proceeded to slide slowly out of the wheelchair. The best that she could do was to grab a hold of my upper body from behind to keep me from sliding right onto the floor. The poor woman started yelling for help and eventually someone did come and help, and clean up the situation. It was a memorable first day of therapy to say the least. I think that was the first time I shit myself; it certainly wouldn't be the last. I also believe that this was when I realized that I had absolutely no control over my bowels and bladder. A year or so before I had my accident, Jennifer's mother's uncle was getting up there in age and he began having bowel problems and one time at a family gathering had an accident and I was amazed at how quick and easy Jenn stepped in, brought him to the bathroom and helped clean him up before anyone even noticed. I was in shock. She said: "the body is just a shell that carries your soul." As much as I thought that I personally could handle any crisis situation, I know I wouldn't have handled it, forget about being that smooth so as not to create a scene to preserve this man's dignity. She was as cool and calm as I've ever seen her. I guess it was a premonition. I mention this only because this moment flashed in my head as I lay there waiting to get cleaned up. I felt like an old man unable to control his bowels. Mentally I understood that I was not an old man, but a young man with a spinal cord injury and was unable

THE ACCIDENT

to control his body. Emotionally I felt like that older man. The hardest part was when two strangers come and clean you up. As much as they try to alleviate the situation, all I could do was close my eyes and wait for it to be over. I was so embarrassed. Even the bed baths, which is supposed to be every man's dream, was an almost unbearable experience. I've always been a private person, never liked to be touched, unless of course I wanted to be. This was totally different. This felt wrong, 'just close your eyes and it'll be over soon'.

Therapy became the next thing to look forward to, even though I was bedridden still, it was some kind of physical exercise and I was always up for that. Even back then I was determined to get back some kind of return, I vowed to walk again. This was me, 'can't nothing hold me back, except me'. There was this older head nurse, nurse Fran, who tried to give me a dose of tough love and told me that she had seen several spinal cord injury patients and that she had never seen anyone regain the ability to walk. I looked her dead in the eyes and said: "my name is Francisco Luis Fernandes and I'll be your first". It's a common emotional reflex among those who become paralyzed. They believe that they'll walk again. I mean who hasn't heard the story of the person who was in an accident, paralyzed, and then walked out of the hospital weeks later. I was sure that was me. My brother Joe even brought in a newspaper clipping of a man who was paralyzed seven years and one day started wiggling his toes, then his legs and eventually began to walk. What an inspirational story, I would do the same; I vowed it to myself as well as to my wife. My poor brother was absolutely beside himself. Actually he didn't know what to do with himself, coming to visit me in the middle of the night. He felt so helpless. As for nurse Fran, I now understand the point she was trying to convey to me. Accept my situation, move on with my life and find something to do with the rest of my life. The only problem was: my name is Francisco Luis Fernandes and I can't accept that I'll never walk again. That I'll never build another sand castle with Jenn again, never hold my wife's hand or gently tickle her with my fingers again, never shoot a good game of pool again, never play basketball again, never brush my teeth again without struggling, never swing a baseball bat again. A BASEBALL BAT. I'm sorry, I'm not stupid, I understand my situation but I'll never ACCEPT this. It's just another challenge. Work hard, be smart, get to know all about paralysis, be tenacious and never ever give up. Your life has been in preparation for this, all of life is a learning experience. Up until June 17th intuitively I felt winds of change coming in my life, I could smell it. I didn't think it was this. This was the complete opposite of what I was expecting, or was it. If it's one thing life has taught me is that it never goes in the direction that you envision, which is not a bad thing necessarily and what you learn most is usually through adversity, so don't be afraid of it, in fact don't be afraid of anything. That's what Nietzsche wrote. Embrace adversity; don't waste your life in constant effort to avoid it. It's a waste of time and energy to regret any experience of life. So this would be it, my torch to carry. Don't know how long it would take, hopefully not too long (silly me, any lesson worth learning takes time). After being told 'you can't do that' my entire youth had prepared me as a young adult that I would never take NO for an answer. Find a way, no matter how and what it takes, find a way. It's a lesson that is with me every day, every hour, every minute. Anticipation is the key to my life, visualization, seeing it in my mind before doing it, right down to the simplest task. That and don't whine about it, another waste of time and it's bad for the spirit. Can't stand whiners.

Speaking of whiners, I briefly had a roommate after I had come out of I.C.U. that me and Jenn named 'Aching Ernie' who was having a slipped disc operated on. I'm not one to complain or make a fuss, it's just in my nature and now I'm in this position where I'm reliant on someone else for just about everything, but enough about me..... for now. Ernie was a trip. This man didn't stop talking from the moment he arrived to the moment he left. Here he is complaining to me, to me, (which I would later realize would become a reoccurring theme from others) how much pain he was in, why was this happening to him, he's so scared. Wah wah wah wah wah. I honestly felt sorry for his blind ignorance. It was the first time I thought to myself, "can you even hear yourself and do you realize how stupid you sound complaining to me?" Some people just love to complain, what a simply ironic oxymoron. Aching Ernie needed more morphine than one man could possibly ever need, the nurses even said so. You'd swear his entire body was broken. As for me, I didn't want anything to do with any pain killing dope. I finally got my body clean and sober, if I'm not in excruciating pain, I can suck it up and deal. I don't ever want to be an Ernie.

After some work, I began sitting in a wheelchair with regularity and thoroughly enjoyed physical therapy, although at this point it was only from my bed. It was exciting to see what muscles I had and which one's I didn't according to the bundle of nerves that comes from C5 and C6. I had biceps but very little triceps (2 on the right and 1 on the left on a scale of 1 to 5, 5 being the strongest). This is determined through a series of meticulous tests, checking motor and sensation throughout your entire body. That's another funny thing about spinal cord injuries, it's unique in that any two individuals may have identical fractures at the same vertebrae and yet one may have the use of their hands and the other not, one with closed fisted hands (like mine), the other with an open palm. Just depends on the nerves that were damaged, it's crazy. As an able bodied man I was athletic and worked out on a regular basis. I had no idea how important each muscle group unto itself is. Now this was another challenge, my triceps were flickering, which means that there some signal going to that muscle group, but was lost and confused. Now I would work on my triceps and show them the way, in fact it was just a way to channel my attention in a neurotic, yet positive direction.

Next came the 4th of July and all we wanted to do was eat a hot dog outside. Just to feel the warmth of the sun on my face, smell fresh air that wasn't regulated or air conditioned. Because of the holiday they were on a limited

THE ACCIDENT

nursing staff and they couldn't afford any extra help. I believe that this was one of the first times I felt truly disabled and the rules that apply to able bodied people didn't always apply to me. Not trying to sound either bitter or negative and not that I'm complaining, it's just a fact. Anyway we had to settle on a window that was down the hall within eyesight. It overlooked the entire hospital yard and halfway down the street. What a beautiful day, not cloud in the sky. Looking out I could see people walking down the sidewalk, pushing strollers: "Do they even know how lucky they are?" and then I see it. A young boy riding his bike and I wonder if I'll ride again and reality hits me over the head like a baseball bat and I start balling uncontrollably. Finally Jenn begins to cry, we hold each other, never saying a word. Radar love. Pulling ourselves together we make the best of the situation, which is all you can ever really do. That was how we spent our first holiday together after my accident, definitely a memorable one.

My overall stay at St. Francis Hospital was nice. The nursing staff was personable and kind. Doctor Geranimal was sincere and made it a point to check up on me with regularity. There was this nurses aide named Charles who became a true friend to me, he was a man of faith and was always positive and full of optimism. He used to shave me regularly, and on my last night he was to meet me for my final shave together, except he never showed, and I was sad because I really wanted to say 'goodbye'. To my surprise I was woken up in the middle of the night by Charles, who had been running late on his rounds but was now there for me. Most would've just skipped over me, I mean it was late night, and logically I probably would be sleeping, but he gave me his word that he would be there and he was. He was never afraid to get personal with me, always gave me a listening ear, and after spending more than his allotted time with me that last night, he filled me with hope and promised to email me when I get home. What a beautiful soul that man is.

I spent 19 days there and Jenn never left my side, day in day out, all day and every night. I can't even imagine what life would have been like if she were not there. She was the calm to my storm, I was so spoiled.

Now the trip back home to N.Y.C., getting transferred to Mt. Sinai, was a trip in itself. First of all, the ride was 3 hours and at this point I wasn't able to sit fully upright for more than 15 minutes, so I laid down on a stretcher facing out the back of the ambulance. I had one window to look out of so I was trying to read highway signs. I was so excited to get back to the city. I felt like a fish out of water. Having been born and raised in Danbury, Ct. which is south western Connecticut, just over the New York border and 45 minutes away from Manhattan, from the age of 19 driving into the city was 'the thing to do' and I couldn't wait to move there. Most of my friends thought I was crazy, but to me the 'feel' of New York was for me. The thrill of 'something can happen at anytime, life teetering on the brink of chaos, the hustle and bustle, the shut up and lets go, everything you could ever imagine and you'll find it, the cops got better things to worry about than little o you'. To me it is the greatest city in the world.

THE ACCIDENT

It wasn't until I met Jennifer that my dream of living there came to fruition. We met in 1992, and within a year we moved to the east village in Manhattan. We both applied (me because of her) and got accepted to the School of Visual Arts. As I mentioned before, our friends thought we were mad when we got a job at the school store. We lived together, went to school together and worked together. Now this might seem unhealthy, and under most circumstances it more than likely is, but it really was like being with my best friend. We both hate to lose at anything, right down to playing Hangman, are each others worst critic, and yet are honest enough with each other to take criticism. We were smart enough to each have other friends, who usually wind up hanging out at our apartment, probably because Jenn always had some project for everyone to do, just add alcohol and a good time is sure to happen. Hell, living in the east village, sitting on our front steps and people watching was a blast, forget about the memories we had on our roof. Since the front lobby door was always locked, you needed a key or someone to buzz you in to enter, so myself, Jenn and our buddy Pete, who I went to film school with, would spend hours at night either yelling out to anyone who walked down the block, or throwing macaroni salad at any prostitute that pretended to 'just be walking down our street'. We literally owned 12th street, and people got the message, because they either walked on the opposite side of the street or we would see them avoid our street all together. What a great city, I was lucky to have such a cool girl to share it with. My previous experiences with girlfriends were that they were, for the most part, always clingy. Jenn was the girl that had her own thing going on. I loved it and I didn't mind sharing my life. Now living in 'Gotham' the world seemed at our feet. Did I mention that I loved living in The City?

The ride seemed to have taken forever and the paramedic who was in the back with me started looking a little nervous. We were getting close. These guys never go into the city and are definitely not used to the pace of traffic. I can see the amount of cars behind us increase and the road is getting bumpy. I recognize the Brooklyn Queens Expressway and I know we are close. No one says anything to me, but I believe we got lost because I hear the driver is asking Jenn for directions. After awhile we arrive and everything is getting a little bit crazy. The long marathon is finishing with a sprint to the end. Before I knew it I was out of the ambulance. I squinted my eyes, the sun stared directly at me, the warmth of it felt wonderful but was quickly squelched as I was wheeled into the hospital and rushed down a hallway. There were so many people in the hallway we were having a hard time navigating down it and no one was getting out of the way or helping out with directions. What most people who don't live in or around Manhattan don't realize about New Yorkers is that they are not necessarily rude but they usually have 90 minutes of work to do in an hour and that there's very little to no time to deviate from that course, nothing personal. That's what happens when you cram 1.5 million people onto an island that's 22.7 square miles (that's a population density of 66,940 people per square mile, not including commuters). The next thing I notice is that the ceiling is crooked and cracked all over the place, as opposed to St. Francis

THE ACCIDENT

which is probably 50 years younger and much more aesthetically pleasing. To me the cracks remind me of lines on an old mans face, much more character and tells of his many travels. I half laugh to myself, 'I'm home' but my amusement is only temporary when I get wheeled to my room. Instead of a quiet, cozy room with one roommate, I now had a tiny room with three roommates, and man was it loud. I had forgotten how loud everything was. Now my three roommates were all older men, none with spinal cord injuries and all were staring at me with my huge neck brace on. They transferred me onto my bed and the ambulance drivers that drove us there were out before I could even thank them. For some reason they had to adjust my bed for something and I had to be sat up. The nursing aide assigned to 'care' for me I will never forget. His name is Julius. He is Haitian and is a very friendly man, not very careful though. You see at this point in my post injury life, I didn't even know how to hold myself upright, something as simple as just putting my arms out to help stabilize myself is foreign to me. I just know that if I'm not held onto strong enough I will just flop over, and that's something I'm still coming to grips with, that if I'm not careful I could just fall over like an infant. When you're constantly in a bed your safe, no threat of falling over and for the most of my stay at the other hospital, I stayed in bed. Now here is Julius, a relatively large man, whose holding me with one outstretched arm and not really paying that much attention to me, chatting it up with the other guys in the room. I tell him again to hold onto me, which he assures me he is and just like that I fall over. I hit my head against the wall and begin to scream bloody murder, spitting out every profanity that I had in my vocabulary, insulting him and his job skills, and he couldn't shut me up. Believe me he tried and I wasn't letting up until someone else knew of his ineptitude, then in walked the head nurse with Jenn. If they thought I was screaming bloody murder before, wait to they get a load of Jenn. She was my personal pit bull and wouldn't even think twice of tearing down a floor before getting the results that I needed, to a fault I must admit, but it was always for my well being. After day one everyone knew who we were. I guess we sure know how to make an entrance. That's another thing I would later come to understand, that a nursing staff is like a fraternity in itself, there was always a veteran who had been there forever and was always real nice and made the time to get to know you and your situation, how your doing and yet be quick and efficient, when they make their rounds to take your vital signs four times a day. Then there was the new nurse who always needed help and was never sure of herself and never got personal, she was on a schedule. Of course there was a 'Nurse Ratched' who never said more than two words to you, and always seemed to be crabby. Yet if something, anything happened during the course of the day the whole staff knew about it, from the day to the night shift, even the aides knew, and they all knew that I hit my head that first day. Needless to say Julius kissed my ass for my entire stay there; he actually turned out to be a pretty cool guy. He was in his 50's but looked my age and had worked at the hospital since he first came to America when he was 18, and was going to retire early; The American dream. He talked to everyone and anyone who would listen, this guy was a character, he was funny too, so me

THE ACCIDENT

and Jenn named him: Orange Julius. That's another thing, I'm not quite sure when we started doing it, it couldn't have been too long after we met but we started our own way of categorizing individuals, objects and events with a separate yet similar word or small phrase. I'm sure it sounds stupid, but really it's a quick way to reference a memory without going into long term detail of who, what and when. Just 'hey remember Orange Julius' is all that's needed to recall that memory.

Now that the whole Orange Julius fiasco is behind us, I get situated in my bed, hang up my personal shrine, dinner comes, Jenn gets into bed and feeds me and reality starts to kick in. Now that we're back home in New York, Jenn's going to be leaving me at night to sleep in her own bed, feed the cats and god forbid go back to work. Now this wasn't a newsflash where it took us by surprise, we both discussed this ahead of time. Yes it would be difficult for me being in a hospital over night by myself without my security blanket, I had been so spoiled up to this point, now was a real test, not only for me but Jenn had to go home alone for the first time and face her reality, 'home is a cold lonely place' she would later tell me. Difficult times for both of us lay ahead and we both knew it. Visiting hours are until 8pm and of course that doesn't apply to Jenn, she would stay until she was ready and no nurse or anybody would tell her otherwise. After a good solid cry she pulls the curtain around me and then leaves and it's dark outside so I tell her to catch a cab. I'm not there to protect her, but I can't dwell on that now. She's gone and I feel so alone, the absolute loneliest feeling that I've ever felt. It's so loud and I just want to fall asleep so the night can be over, but of course that doesn't happen and I do everything that I possibly can do not to get all panicky and stuff. I envision myself walking, nothing special or anything just walking. That's the trick or the trigger, I later come to understand, that this is a technique that soothes an individual to relax, stop anxious thoughts, allowing his or her brain waves to slow down to an alpha brain wave, which sleep then follows. Of course this is all hindsight I was just acting on instinct, which I would have to perform many times that first night, between the noise and my own fear, it felt as though I was awake most of the night.

The next morning was one of the hardest I've ever felt. Now I must admit I've never been a morning person, but waking up to a ruckus from the nursing staff, no Jenn, and oh yeah my spasms were at their worst first thing in the morning. Now for anybody who is unfamiliar with those who have spinal cord injuries and have spasms, they vary in degree but for the most part they are pretty violent. The old saying 'if you don't use it you lose it' is so absolutely true, without getting into technical terms, if you don't move your legs the signals get lost and your legs, or even abdominal muscles, in fact any muscle group that's paralyzed, release that energy in a strong violent jerking motion. They can even knock you right out of your wheelchair and usually freak most people out, seeing your legs shake like that looks so unnatural. Some have spasms and nerve pain, which thankfully I didn't have. Waking up with spasms was horrible, I'll never forget this poor nurse came to me, must've been 6'oclock in the morning, to give

THE ACCIDENT

me my bed bath. She couldn't have weighed more than a hundred pounds and all of 5'4" and she leaned over me. What the previous 19 days taught me was that spasms were at an all time worst first thing in the morning and me being half asleep was trying to convey this point to her, (it usually takes at least two people to hold my legs down until the spasms release and subside), I obviously didn't do a good job. I was lying on my back and as she uncovered my legs, my knees shot straight up towards my chests and clocked her straight in the jaw with a solid 'thud'. It was as if someone just unloaded a strong right cross to her poor fragile head. I felt so bad and apologized repeatedly. She didn't say much, don't think she could, but she did finish her job like the good soldier that she was. I gained much respect for nurses and aides after that. I was still so much in shock that this happened to me. I can't believe that I can't move my body. I've always hated hospitals; I can't believe I have to stay here. I just want to go home and close my eyes and everything will be alright. It reminds me of a time when I was 9 and me and my big brother Joe caused my sister to get bit by our neighbor's dog and had to go to the emergency room. Me and Joe had to wait in the car and all I could do is close my eyes and wish that everything was alright, which of course it wasn't, but I was always a dreamer and even at 29 I was still that little boy.

Next on the mornings agenda came the doctor on duty surrounded by his group of interns, all trying to stand out among their peers in front of him as they go from patient to patient doing their rounds. They're all dressed in their white lab coats, all looked the same, and stood six feet away from you as they discuss your situation out loud, then take two steps to their left and talk to you as if you didn't just hear every single word they just said. I felt like an animal in a zoo. The morning nurse had pulled back the curtain and now breakfast has arrived. I had a clear view of my neighbors as they all tore into their own. I looked at mine and thought: "great, what am I supposed to do now!" At this point I couldn't even raise my own bed so I could sit up and at least see what I had, forget about trying to figure out how to go about eating it. In walked Orange Julius and he came to my aid first, to the chagrin of the others. He always catered to me first and never hesitated to yell at the others. He did a lot to make me feel better. I seemed to be in a room filled with older men. One guy was yelling in Spanish at any nurse who walked in our room, the other kept belly aching about not being able to move his bowels and the last was an old man who must've had trouble hearing because he was on the phone all morning speaking loudly. He kept referring to me as the new kid who has a horse collar, meaning my huge neck brace, which I guess does resemble a horse collar, at least that's how it felt. I wait for a nurse to come in and ask her to close my curtain. I can't wait until Jenn gets here. Be careful what you wish for, right? I couldn't wait to get back to Manhattan. Coming from a smaller hospital that was attentive and was always within earshot of your needs, now if I need anything it takes twice as long, understandably why, too many patients not enough staff, again I was spoiled, there's a lesson here. Another thing about being back in Manhattan, I was expecting to see more of my

THE ACCIDENT

friends who couldn't drive to Poughkeepsie. It's a funny thing when you encounter a life altering accident. The friends that you'd think will be there for you are not always; at least this was my experience. Jenn had told me that she had gotten a hold of many of my school friends, people I worked with, she even unselfishly got a hold of my 'first love' Kristen, who I had always spoken well of because she was there for me as a kid during my tough childhood. When Jenn called her and introduced herself and then explained what had happened to me, her only response was: "He got married"? She promised to come and visit which of course she never did. Maybe I thought too much of our friendship, obviously she didn't, when her only concern was not for my well being but whether I was married or not. I of course had no reason to doubt Jenn, I had no idea she was calling many of my 'old time' friends. Some came just once promising to return, which once again didn't happen. I can't tell you what these people were thinking, I just know they weren't thinking of me and putting their own selfishness aside. People are so weird; at least the animal kingdom is more predictable. My own mother came to visit me just once, in a wheelchair! When this happened I'm not sure, since I saw her just a few weeks before and she was walking around. My mother always had the habit of having physical ailments that doctors could never diagnose. All through my youth, right down to the day I got married, she suddenly had some kind of condition and didn't attend her son's wedding. Me personally, I wouldn't let death keep me from my child's marriage, but that's just me. I was even the first child in my family to get married; at least my bastard father attended that. So here is my mother, sitting in her wheelchair next to my bed and she proceeds to stand up all 'wobbly like', as if she had been in that chair for years. She tells me, "If I can do it than you can too" such pearls of wisdom. 'Except I have a spinal cord injury and you have....well like nothing, thanks, thanks a lot'! I swore to myself that I would never be that person.

After speaking with my physical and occupational therapist, we set up a schedule and finally I had something else to look forward to, regaining my independence. Dinner comes and I'm excited, I'm already sitting up, so I give it a go and see how far I can get before help comes and Jenn would be here soon as well, I'd impress her. Loving a challenge, my problem solving skills kick in. Starting with the plastic spork in the encased clear bag, I hold it between my wrists. I have enough strength in each wrist and shoulders to hold it tight and that's when I discovered that my teeth would become my fingers, tearing and opening packages. It was actually easier than what I thought. With determination and patience I managed to get the school-like cardboard milk box open, still no one has come in. It may sound silly but something so trivial as this gave me such a feeling of self satisfaction. All I needed to do was get the top off of the plate, which I eventually did and guess what the main course was ....spaghetti. I had no idea how to hold my spork without gripping it, forget about spaghetti. I can tell you that it didn't go well, but it's actually easier and more entertaining to hear it from Jenn's perspective, as this moment in our lives she recalls often. This is how she saw it:

THE ACCIDENT

"As I entered the hospital room, I knew it was dinner time but was not prepared for what I would see when I drew back the curtain. Cisco was in his bed sitting up, tray in front of him and the saddest, most defeated look on his face. I had never seen that expression before and as my eyes panned down to his chest I understood why. There was spaghetti and sauce all over the place. From the looks of it not one piece of spaghetti had made it into his mouth. I was so heartbroken for him that I started to cry but at the same time I had never been so proud. He had actually tried to eat a meal on his own for the very first time. After the initial shock of the scene I just witnessed, I was more proud than sad, so we cleaned up the mess and started over. This time we cut the spaghetti first and I helped to keep it on the fork. I will never forget that moment and the emotion I felt."

Chapter Three

REHAB AND BEYOND

Her name is Jennifer, she is all of 5'2" and is as strong as a bull and is one of the most patient, empathetic and encouraging persons I have ever met and she is my second of many physical therapists. Another girl named Jennifer forever in my life who I owe so much to that I can never repay. Her impact on my post spinal cord injury life I wouldn't even realize until many months later. We started off slowly. A tilt table was the first assignment of the day, which is exactly what it sounds like, a padded table that you get strapped onto. Your whole body starts from a lying down position then slowly tilts upright twenty five degrees and you hold in that position for five to ten minutes. Blood pressure is constantly monitored and Jennifer is watching my eyes and gives me pointers, like waiving my arms and doing deep breathing techniques to keep yourself from passing out, and a sip of water helps too. She helped me recognize the symptoms as they approached: first comes the light headed feeling, then ringing in the ears, then the tunnel vision, followed by complete weakness, even lifting your head is impossible, passing out is the final outcome. Then someone shakes you awake and you're left wondering what just happened. Now I have been given some tools to live by, ones that helped me create strategies to help overcome my disability. First is the recognition of these symptoms as they first begin, I still use them today. These were the first of many tools I was given by Jennifer in our rehab sessions. Mat mobility was next on the agenda for the day, where laying out a physical therapy mat and simply seeing what I can or can't do, rolling myself over, sitting straight legged on the mat while holding myself up. After that we progressed to me sitting at the edge of the mat, legs dangling off, just holding myself up with my arms, elbows locked out, head back and squeezing my shoulder blades together just to keep my own balance (which is the first step in being independent). It was exhausting, I couldn't believe it. So much energy for such a minimal task, I was so distraught. Being 5'9", 175 pounds, I was short and stocky but prided myself on being strong, no powerful is more like it. I remember carrying two cases of beer up a flight of stairs in the middle of a Friday night frenzy when I worked at the bar. I did it like it was nothing. Now I'm shaking like a leaf, straining every fiber of my being just to hold myself up from falling over. I last about twenty seconds. My therapist Jennifer kept telling me to be patient, she would tell me that she could see that my fight was strong but that

I kept thinking as though I was still able bodied. I would have to let that way of thinking go and think backwards, not to dwell on what used to be easy, but what can I do now and what can I accomplish during my three months that I was going to stay at The Mount Sinai Hospital. She is a die hard Mets fan, which we'd usually fight about what team was better in New York, which of course is a ridiculous argument because twenty six World Championships speak for themselves, but we spoke a familiar language and a game plan was formed for our therapy sessions. Oddly it turned out later that October, that the Yankees played the Mets in the World Series, the 'subway series' which naturally the Yankees won four games to one. Unfortunately I had been discharged almost two months earlier and didn't have the heart to go and visit her to rub it in. We did go to the parade though and for the first time in my life the police treated me with respect and without prejudice. In fact they went out of their way to bring me front row to watch the floats go by and the entire team saw me and waived directly to me, even Rudy Giuliani looked directly at me and gave me a 'thumbs up' signal with his hand. Jenn was star struck for the moment and didn't take the picture, I just laughed, the memory is always better anyway.

It was about this time when I started going to physical and occupational therapy regularly that I started noticing something......interesting. The nurses aides did most of the grunt work, helping the patients with their bowel routine, (mine was scheduled for 6 a.m. every other morning which sucked because I was never a morning person and could never take a shit first thing in the morning but I had no choice in the matter), showering and dressing us. I kid you not this one time after my routine I was to take a shower and my aide was juggling too many patients at one time and left me alone for a while sitting in my shower chair. I began to hear the ringing in my ears, softly at first, and then loud and despite my efforts I knew what was going to happen next, everything went black. I awoke some time later and I was still alone, thank god I had my seatbelt on. I was freaked out that this happened and started screaming that bloody murder that I so love to do when necessary. Needless to say she never worked my section anymore. The 'interesting' part was when, after I was all ready for therapy, the nurse on duty would come in with a couple of male aides and after they'd transfer me into my wheelchair the nurse would bend down and put my shoes on. Now I swear I'm no pervert and I love my wife to death, and would never even flirt with another now, especially after everything that's happened in our lives in the past few weeks, Jenn was so faithful, how could I not be the same? But I am a man, which is no excuse, but I couldn't help but see what I saw. The cute little Miss Nurse on duty this particular day was wearing a lower cut shirt and when she went to put my sneakers on I just so happened to look down and saw straight down her shirt. I was so embarrassed that I looked away real quick, hoping that she didn't see me, which she didn't. I saw another girls bra, I felt like a school kid all over again, I laughed to myself. After this day I made sure not to 'sneak a peak' because the nurses are usually talking to you and you do not want to get caught, every nurse on every duty would know about it by days end, as I mentioned before if one nurse knows of something that's happened during the course of the day then they all will eventually know. It's just not worth it. Keeping on the subject, there's the Light Gate physical therapist who was from England. Now my physical therapy is during the day and Jenn worked so she never got a chance to see me, except for this day. This was my first day to use the Light Gate, which is basically a treadmill with a frame over it. I was strapped into a harness and suspended over it as two therapists each grab a foot and simulate a walking motion, and a third therapist stands behind me to keep my balance. Studies have shown that this therapy can help promote the nerve signal from the brain get to the legs, especially during the first few weeks of a spinal cord injury. Honestly to me it's a crap shoot. S.C.I. in each individual situation is unique and their outcome may or may not be the same as yours. I was excited because not only was Jenn there but my brother Joe took the day off too and was there for my support. The session started off, and I thought good and hard about moving those legs, swinging my arms in opposition to my legs, I had never thought of that before. As you step with your right leg your left arm swings to counter balance your weight and the beautiful ballet of walking upright is achieved. Jenn was so excited for me until the therapist switched places; it was demanding work for them as well in their defense. Jenn realized the female English therapist was going to be the one behind me and she had just worked up a sweat moving my left leg so she took off her outer shirt which left her wearing only her thin undershirt. Now she was no skinny little therapist and when taking a break she would lean me against herself, nothing inappropriate, I was just resting against her, but boy would Jenn stare at me as if I had something to do with this. My brother laughed his ass off and swore he was going to attend every therapy session and Jenn to this day still talks about that therapist and her white lace bra. She made sure that she didn't miss one Light Gate session.

    The next couple of weeks flew by and I saw improvement in my strength and stamina but my legs weren't cooperating with the Light Gate sessions and no significant improvement was assessed so my sessions discontinued. I was crushed and became depressed, I felt wronged and dwelled on how shitty my life was. That night I was inconsolable and Jenn knew it, she didn't say a word she just crawled into my bed and held me as we watched T.V. sharing the earphones. It was getting late and I was dreading her leaving me that night. What came on next made both of our jaws drop, it was a commercial for the following show and it was about Christopher Reeve. Jenn didn't care about staying an extra hour longer. She was just as excited about watching the show as I was. I am forever a comic book geek and remember seeing Superman the movie as a kid and Christopher Reeve became my hero. I was still able bodied when he had his unfortunate accident, and my ears would always perk up whenever there was anything about him on T.V. and now that I had my spinal cord injury he became my hero on a personal level, he was tenacious and passionate, never afraid to be himself. The show was about stem cells and their possibilities, which was my first exposure to the subject. The cameras followed him around as he did his workout routine. He understood the importance of maintaining a strong body and his workouts were long and tough everyday. The part that still stays with me still to this day is when I saw him on the Light Gate. Now Christopher Reeve had broken his neck at C2 and although we were both considered quadriplegics, his level of injury was far greater than mine is. He couldn't even lift his arms to swing them while on the Light Gate and I swear it's as if he spoke to me directly through the television and I thought to myself: "shut up and quit feeling sorry for yourself"! That's the man of steel there, he soldiers on going forward, never back and I had no right to feel the way I did, *it could always be worse.* Jenn hugged me long and hard, kissed me goodnight and went home to research everything there was online about stem cells, what a girl.

After about two months I started to feel really home sick. I missed my home, my neighborhood, and my two cats. I wanted out. I was beginning to feel as though I was ready for the real world. My therapist Jennifer thought I should stay as long as I could, but she saw it in my eyes that I was wanting out and so she started the final preparations for my leaving. She had to see if I was going to leave in a power chair or a manual wheelchair. Now the first time I used a power chair I cried, I felt so disabled, helpless even. Using a manual chair I at least felt more 'normal' if that makes any sense. I also liked that it was more difficult to push yourself, but it built endurance and strength. Using a power chair had its advantages too. I never needed any assistance what so ever and I could go anywhere I wanted in a quick and efficient way. There was this time after therapy when I was in a power chair and I left my floor without permission to go outside and meet Jenn. She was on her way to come visit me after work. I remember feeling the warmth of the sun on my face and the noises of the traffic, the real world, man how I missed it. Being secluded inside the confines of the hospital and never going outside feels like another world and you live it for so long that you forget what it's like in the outside world. Being outside all alone, the nurses would've killed me if they knew it but it felt great breaking the rules and it was for a genuine purpose, I was going to surprise Jenn. I couldn't wait. After some time I saw her from a distance get off the bus and head towards the hospital. She didn't even see me. Why would she, she certainly wasn't expecting to see me, but as she came closer she saw me and began crying and rushed to me and gave me the biggest hug ever. I asked her why she was crying and Jenn said it was because not only did I surprise her but that I looked so independent, she was so proud of me. I knew I was going to get in trouble when I returned to my room from the nursing staff, but it was all worth it just to see Jenn's face. After that day I wasn't so against owning a power chair so I picked out both a manual and power chair from a catalog, it's smart to be prepared for any situation. The manual I would use on a daily basis indoors, need to build stamina, and the power chair I could use for times that I would be outside for long distances, like going to the Bronx Zoo, the Atlantic City boardwalk..... I would, later on, set my chair to its maximum setting and fly up and down the boardwalk as I tow Jenn as she holds onto a bungee cord that's attached to the back of my chair while wearing her roller skates. People always get a laugh as they watch us fly by and Jenn too is usually laughing out loud. It's one of her favorite things to do and once again I'm getting ahead of myself, sorry.

With everything ordered the final step was to say goodbye, which we did in a special way. It was Jenn's idea but she let me take all the credit. She had bought a dozen roses and we went around and handed them to all of my P.T.'s and special nurses that were so kind to me and of course my favorite physical therapist Jennifer. Her only bit of advice: "don't go home and lay in bed and get fat"! I thought that was crazy, but I'm sure she must've seen it a hundred times before and as time would prove, it was some excellent advice.

I was so excited..... I'm finally going home, and I could see that Jenn was just as excited. We boarded the ambulette along with a half dozen others and the ride seemed to take forever. This was the first time I was in a motor vehicle since my accident and I was all over the place, so I held onto my wheelchair with all my might. Ours of course was the last stop, but it was great seeing the neighborhood again and then there it was, our front door. I was lucky that we lived on the ground floor because wheelchairs and stairs don't get along. I'll never forget the range of emotions I felt the moment I was wheeled into our apartment that day. First was excitement, the familiar smell of our individual apartment, then happiness as Mickey and Mallory, our two cats greeted us at the door. It might be me but it almost seemed as they were confused upon seeing me in a wheelchair. They kind of walked around me at first and then up to me for their petting, but like I said it might be just me. Then everything hit me all at once, the ladder in the living room still stood there from before when I used it to paint the brick wall. I had air brushed our entire living room wall which was at least twenty feet long, brick by brick, shading various ones to give it an authentic look. I took great pride in that wall, it came out better than I had thought, and everyone thought I was crazy to do this by hand. I considered it a project of patience, like a good Tibetan monk. When seeing that ladder I broke down and started balling my eyes out, no thoughts ran through my head just pure emotion. Jenn had already set up our apartment so that it was totally accessible for me. She even knocked out a wall of the shower so that I can wheel right into it. It felt wonderful being home but part of me felt like a stranger in a strange land, and all of that optimism I felt leaving the hospital turned to sadness because this was it, this is my reality. I got into bed and that was it, I never wanted to get out, pull the covers over my head and wish the world away.

Unfortunately Jenn still had to go to work and we had to find a home aide for me for the daytime which became a fiasco. The first guy the agency sent over was all of a hundred and fifty pounds. I doubted he could transfer me to my wheelchair, and when asked he agreed, he had no experience helping someone in a wheelchair before and he could barely speak English. We looked at each other and knew that this wasn't going to work and he didn't even last the day. It was nothing personal, I just have specific needs and was not going to settle for just anyone that they sent, this is my life we're talking about and normally I don't like to make a fuss, but there are exceptions to the rule. Needless to say it became a long drawn out process of finding an aide that was both professional and experienced. Approximately two weeks and nine home aids later the agency sent over Alicia and said if she didn't work out that we would have to find another agency. We were stuck between a rock and a hard place because I was to begin physical therapy at home for three months followed by outpatient rehab. We agreed to give her a week, see if she was helpful with my therapy and take it from there. Alicia turned out just fine; thankfully, she wasn't shy and got down on the floor right with me during my therapy sessions with Benjamin, a big strong man, my kind of therapist. Not really knowing too much about spinal cord injuries he basically wanted me to build endurance, sitting on the floor and see how long I can hold myself up without using my hands, stuff like that. The only problem was that right after therapy I'd get right back into bed where it was safe and comfortable, no stress, which of course didn't help with my endurance and of course I gained weigh, Jennifer was right. Then there was the time Jenn came home from work and there I was as usual in bed watching T.V. and she said: "one day I'd like to come home and not see my husband in bed" and it shook me to the core. Not only because it was true but because she referred to me as her 'husband' which of course I was but was so wrapped up in my own drama that I forgot her needs. The next day I made sure I was in my chair when she got home and she was so happy. I was lucky to find a girl who was happy with the simple things in life.

I was beginning to feel hopeless and started to grow a beard. I swore that I would grow it until I started to get some 'return' to my legs: "please god show me a sign, I thought I was special". It wasn't just me in my delusional mind that thought I was special, people would tell me, complete strangers sometimes would make a comment about me being different, New Yorkers are never afraid to speak their mind, good or bad, I love it. There was this one time I was coming home from bartending and it was twilight time, about 6am and the sun was just rising. I was about to get into my car and an older homeless woman asked me for some change which I obliged her with. I mean how could I refuse her when I just made about four hundred dollars and it's burning a hole in my pocket. I remember this occasion vividly because as I handed her the change she looked me dead in the eye real hard and said that "I had Christ in my eyes". Now I had met my share of homeless while living in New York, never avoided them, and never felt bad denying them any change. I always gave according to the individual. For instance, if they are performing anything, any instrument (pots and pans) or just singing even if it's poorly, they're trying and who am I to deny them some pocket change. This older woman was different. She didn't look like a wino so I just felt compelled to give her what little I did and her response didn't feel like a generic expression.

From the look in her eyes she genuinely meant it. It gave me goose bumps.

Now the bargaining with god and the growing of my beard business is a funny story. I had read of stories online of those who had been paralyzed for months sometimes years and had regained the ability to walk again and I was convinced I was one of those individuals. I had learned how precious life is and now I'm ready to return to normal life again. Silly me. Three months go by and I have a beard that would make any redneck real proud. Jenn takes her pictures and I'm even impressed at its length but I'm still not walking. Even Alicia and Benjamin get a kick out of my beard, but to me I was dead serious. The time had come now for me to take my next step in my evolution, outpatient rehabilitation, which to me was scary and I felt I wasn't quite ready for that yet. I knew that I had to shave my beard which I did all by myself with the help a cordless shaver. Besides feeding, shaving myself was the next independent thing I accomplished alone and it felt wonderful again, something as simple as this brought great joy. A flicker of memory crosses my mind, before my injury I used to love grooming myself and Jenn used to kid me that I would take longer than she would when going out. I wasn't a 'pretty boy' or anything; it's more like that 'compulsive' thing. I just enjoyed being clean and neat and the process of doing it felt very rewarding, it was no big deal. At least that's what I used to convince myself. It was one week before I would return to Mount Sinai for outpatient rehab and I was determined to clean and groom myself every morning in the bathroom from my wheelchair like a big boy. Let me start by saying that I have always been one who never liked his picture taken because I've always been overly critical of my looks but Jenn changed all of that with her insistent camera. She'd take a picture of me at any time and I eventually let my guard down and secretly enjoyed my picture to be taken. Since coming home I couldn't even bare to look at pictures of my able bodied self, it hurt so bad and that's just pictures. Staring at myself through the bathroom full size mirror for the first time was unbelievable, I cried so long and so hard, I just couldn't identify myself with the man in the mirror. Again, after allowing me to vent for awhile, Jenn comes from behind and without saying a word just holds me for a short while then grabs the toothpaste and puts it on my electric tooth brush, leaves it on the sink and walks away. I hook my left arm around one push handle behind the back of my wheelchair to stabilize myself, my trunk/core control is still a mess and the balancing act begins as I hold my toothbrush with my right hand. I had learned in therapy how to hold objects without the use of my fingers using a technique called tenodesis, where I have the ability to pull my wrist back and pinch items in my hand and hold them, like my eating utensils. I was lucky I could do this, many with the same level of injury are not able to do this and I feel for them because it's hard to imagine not being able to do even these simple tasks, life was already tough enough but I am truly grateful that I can do what I can do. After my first experience alone in the bathroom a feeling of self satisfaction overcame me, I was so proud of myself. I felt ready for out patient therapy.

Today's the day, I felt like it was my first day at a new school, I was both nervous and excited. This would be the first time I was to go outside since coming home and I was eager to learn more so I can be more independent. Myself, Jenn and my home aide Alicia all got ready and went outside to wait for the Ambulette to come pick us up. This was my first taste of life in a wheelchair in the outside world. Before this day I was safe in my home, safe from the looks and stares from strangers. As we waited at the corner I couldn't help but look at everyone in their cars look and stare at me as they waited for the traffic light to turn. I felt embarrassed as if I did something wrong and looked the fool to be stared at.... and this is Brooklyn for gods sake where you really have to do something special to get that much attention.

The only time I can remember getting that much attention from onlookers was years ago when I was riding my mountain bike downtown to meet my friend who also lived in Brooklyn. I had my headphones on, music blasting, shades on and I was flying making great time. A traffic jam was up ahead so I decided to straddle the solid middle yellow line that separates going traffic from oncoming traffic and I was in the groove, eyes wide open anticipating moves up ahead. The light ahead was yellow and was about to turn red. I decided to go for it and beat the traffic, unfortunately the car on my right thought the same thing, which wouldn't have been a problem, except it was a left turn lane. The car obviously didn't see me and turned left right into me and I hit the front fender and flew over the hood and tumbled to the ground. I was all over the place and laid there for a second. I was shaking like a leaf. I got to my feet and looked myself over making sure everything was still in place and my elbow was all scraped up and bloody and then the pain kicked in. It was about this time that I noticed that traffic going both ways had completely stopped and just about everyone on the sidewalk had stopped and was staring at me, maybe to see if I were alive? I collected myself the best I could, checked out my bike and looked at the driver who I just ran over and it was this old lady and she looked like she was freaked out. I decided to just get on my bike the best I could and ride off, I was hurting so bad, but that's the only time I can recall having been stared at by so many. This time was different, this felt wrong. I didn't do anything to deserve the stares.

Our ride finally arrived and it was packed full of individuals who all had some kind of disability and were all going to Mount Sinai. When we arrived it felt even more like school. There was a line of ambulettes lined up all along the entire hospital like school buses and tons and tons of people in wheelchairs. I felt at home. We went in and registered, Jenn decided to take a rest and sat on my lap. "Wheelchair love" someone called out to us and when looking over it came from the coolest looking guy I'd ever seen in a wheelchair. He introduced himself as Sayquan, he's about my age, has long dread locks, nice new clothes and the coolest wheelchair I've ever seen. In fact after wheeling into the rehab room, which was huge and full of all kinds of workout machines and mats, I saw so many young, good looking people all in wheelchairs, all working out. I definitely felt at home, finally, except everyone was dressed ordinarily, and here I am with my sweat pants and old sneakers. That's all I ever wore since my injury because I was either in bed or in therapy at the hospital or at home. I wasn't used to social settings and I felt like a nerd. I was used to having the newest clothes, Manhattan always has the latest styles and I had to have the latest Nike sneakers. I can't tell you how much I learned from these guys, they showed me that life doesn't stop because of a spinal cord injury. A guy named Carlos, who would later become a good friend of mine, was shot in the back leaving him a paraplegic (I would always kid him because he had the use of his hands) and they never caught the guy who shot him. He was never bitter about it; in fact he is one of the most outgoing persons I've ever met. He just flipped it. He relished in the fact that he attracted attention and flirted with more women than anyone I've ever met. He was disabled for awhile and worked at the hospital running the Do It Now program which was a one hour long, weekly get together. There I learned so much like I wasn't the only one who accidently pissed their pants or realizing that the majority of relationships and marriages end up breaking up. Even paraplegics that live a totally independent life end up in divorce. I was lucky Jenn really meant it when she said "for better or for worse". Still not sure why she sticks around; I surely don't deserve it. I also learned that even though things make take longer, that it is important to do it, anything, by yourself or at least make an effort to do. Your loved ones that are there for you will do it for you if you allow them to and then you'll have people doing all kinds of things for you and there goes any little bit of independent life that you have. A bit of struggle is always good for the soul. Most of all I learned that I wasn't alone and in the disabled community I belonged. One time ago I was afraid to look at an individual that was disabled in any sort of way. I didn't know how to act. I just knew that they wouldn't want pity. Now here I am on the inside looking out, and I realize a couple of things, one is how silly I was for thinking in that way, I just needed to act as if the person who is disabled is just a person....... who happens to be disabled or handicapped. For the record, I once heard an expression to differentiate the disabled from handicapped and I thought it was perfect. When competing in the Olympics, "one plays for hugs while the other plays for medals". My new friends told me to get out in public as soon as possible, go to a movie, go to a restaurant, to the park go anywhere just get out and get over that fear.

I decided to go to a Yankees game. I was excited and so was Jenn. My brother Joe drove and in our excitement we forgot my Baclofen medication which helps relax my muscles that stiffen up when sitting in my chair for extended times. Well it was a hell of a game. My brother was able to get us tickets to the American League Championship Series, Yankees versus the Seattle Mariners. Their manager Lou Pinella, when asked by the media, guaranteed that they would win this game and play game seven back in Seattle. I was new to this paralysis thing and like I mentioned before I forgot my medication, I also didn't look at the weather forecast for the night and it was cold and of course I didn't bring a blanket or anything to keep me warm. It was at this time I realized that my body's temperature doesn't regulate itself and the outside temperature becomes my core temperature. It was so cold my teeth were chattering. I was such a rookie. Physically I was a wreck; emotionally I was on cloud nine. The Yankees were winning by a few runs in the last inning and the Yankees faithful were all yelling in unison: "NO GAME SEVEN, NO GAME SEVEN"!

It took me two days to recover but I would do it again in a heartbeat it was so awesome, what a great first outing. My next excursion wouldn't be as fun, I decided to take my wife out to dinner and needless to say just transferring in and out of the car was eventful, something that with time and practice would eventually get easier. When we got to the restaurant and went in I swear it felt like the entire place came to an abrupt stop and collectively turned their attention towards us. It wasn't just paranoia, you could just see them looking from the corners of your eyes. I just wanted to get to the table and bury my head in a menu. While waiting I couldn't help but look around and see so many just looking at me and then quickly turn away when they notice me looking at them, like I didn't see them. I wouldn't have minded them looking, people are just curious, and if we catch eye contact just flash a smile, don't insult me by looking away. Years later I would construct a method to suite my madness. Anytime I rolled into a public place, a restaurant, a store, movie theater, anywhere, I give everyone a three strike rule: you look at me once, no problem, twice, okay now your pushing it, the third time I catch you staring at me and don't say hi or flash a smile, then I have no problem stopping what I'm doing and turn my complete attention at that individual and stare at them. Believe me no one likes to be stared at by someone in wheelchair. I know that this isn't necessarily a nice thing to do and individually I believe in personal karma and bettering yourself everyday till the day you die, but I know the little bad boy in me will never fully go away and just as long as he doesn't rear his ugly head too often and his actions don't harm anyone, he's alright with me. Besides he serves a purpose and has certainly helped me through this situation, I can't even imagine what life would be like if I was still concerned about people looking at me.

The first couple of months following my accident seemed to take forever, now the first couple of months of outpatient rehab just flew by. The more you have to do the less time you have. I truly understand that now. I was gaining more strength and my therapist Hillary was proud of me telling me I was one of the few quads she ever worked with that was as independent as I was. This week I was learning to transfer myself from my chair to the mat using a sliding board and was having success, I was so proud of myself. Then one day this young kid rolled in and just popped out of his chair and onto the mat, he had a different therapist that hour. I had never seen him before and I looked at Hillary and asked her if he was a quad like me and she said yes, but his body type was very different than mine, he was tall and had long arms which allowed more leverage to clear his wheelchair and transfer without the use of a sliding board. I was blessed with a long torso and shorter arms, not the ideal type for independent pop over transfers. I was like 'to hell with that I'm not going to be the second best quad in therapy' my competitive juices flowed and so we began working on that next. The truth is I could go to physical therapy for an indefinite amount of time so long as I continued to show progress and had a desire to go, which I did; it gave me purpose for the time being. Ironically, after hating hospitals the first 29 years of my life, a hospital, any hospital is where I felt the most comfortable. Flat floors with no carpet, elevators, no stairs and no one looks at you twice if you're in a wheelchair.

Then it happened. It was September 11, 2001 and Jenn was helping me get ready and we were running late, as usual, when we saw on T.V. what was first reported that a small airplane had crashed into the north tower of the World Trade Building. Jenn worked literally one block away, and my ride to therapy was always over the Brooklyn Bridge into Manhattan which stares right at the Twin Towers. We were both eager to finish getting ready so we could check out what happened, Jenn was going to get up close and personal to see the mess. Then the south tower got hit and everything changed. Our mouths hung open out of disbelief. My home aide Alicia started screaming, she wanted to get her children from school which of course we told her she should do. It felt like the end of the world. When would this madness end, it felt like never. I understand that the whole country hurt that day but when it happens in your backyard it feels real personal. I mean we lived just over the Manhattan Bridge in Brooklyn and we could not only see the dark cloud that hung over the city but could smell it as well. We made a large homemade flag with the Pledge of Allegiance written on the white stripes and hung it on our front gate.

Some time soon after this tragedy, when we were all 'trying to get back to normal' my therapy resumed and we made that trip over the Brooklyn Bridge and they were gone, just dark empty space resided there now, and it just looked wrong. I got home and was just hurting, even though I personally didn't know anyone who died. Later that night I was in bed and I just so happened to look over at my digital clock and it was 9:11pm and instinctively I felt compelled to say this prayer: "Father, I'm so sorry for this day, I'm so sorry for all the lives that were lost on this day, please let their souls be free, please help them find peace. Please ease the pain of all the friends and family of all of those that they suddenly left behind and please let justice be done to all those responsible for this horrible day". I didn't think about it before hand and wasn't used to saying prayers, I believe in god just not the conventional western Christian view of god who looks down from above and judges you. To this day every time I see the clock strike 9:11, I say this silent prayer, I can't help it and I wonder if and when I'll stop, will I ever need to? I can't say, I just feel compelled to say it, it's the least I can do.

I guess it was a few months later that I feel like life was beginning to feel mundane and Hillary was going on maternity leave. I wasn't going to start all over with a new physical therapist and Jenn was tired of working just to pay the rent, which was getting harder every month. It was time for change. We both felt it. I was lucky to have Jenn and her family; unlike mine her family was huge. She had four brothers, two sisters, numerous nieces and nephews, cousins and grandparents. Hell they were even close with the local neighbors, in fact when we were first dating we went to Chris and Tammy's wedding, Tammy has been a life long neighbor and friend. The wedding was huge mostly consisting of Jenn's family, and what a blast we had, in fact that was the first time I met Tammy, she was a beautiful bride, and we even ended up dancing together. What a trip those two are, we remain close to this day. What stayed with me was how much fun everyone seemed to be having and how much people went out of their way to make me feel comfortable. Forget about my future in laws who, from Thanksgiving on, our first holiday together, welcomed me as if I was their real son. My mother in law Barbarajean treated me like the mom I'd always wished for. Never a coarse word, always full of love and as many gifts at Christmas any son could wish for, that's who she is to me. As for my father in law Bill, a man of few words, a kind, giving and simple man and the hardest worker I've ever met. When Jenn and I had decided to move to New York City, I needed to make extra cash and her father hired me without any question. He owns his own landscaping business in Bethel, Connecticut for at least some forty something years, his sons ran some of his customers accounts and all I remember telling myself was to never complain and work real hard, my actions will reveal my personality to them. I wanted them to like me. It was the hardest job that I have ever worked and it was just for the summer. I wished for rain just to get a day off. That summer I mostly worked with Jenn's brother Billy. We got to know each other pretty well. He treated me as if I were his real brother instead of an employee. I certainly appreciated this and I hold a special place in my heart for him always. It was such a foreign feeling, a large family who barely knows me, to welcome me into their home and business with no questions asked, no judgment. My guard came down, Billy helped with that, and I began to allow myself to be accepted as a member of this huge family. It was a comforting feeling belonging to this Ellis family, my birth family was so small and disconnected, so much animosity over the stupidest things resulting in 'this person doesn't talk to that one'. So much dysfunction so little time. Now don't get me wrong Jenn's family has their share of dysfunction, like every family on the face of this planet, but they always got together every holiday, always greeted each other, and despite any argument they always communicated eventually with each other until an understanding was worked out. Even if it's they agreed to disagree, they still communicated with each other. This was a foreign concept to me and was refreshing to know that this behavior among family was possible. I had never been exposed to anything like this before and I thank them for it. They always think it's no big deal, but it's because they know no better, they just behave the way they do because that's just the way it is. If you ask me, like any professional sports team, or even a business, everything ultimately starts with the very top or head and in this case it's Mr. Bill Ellis. He is the rock.

As I mentioned before, we both felt a need for a change and it was at this point that Jenn's parents just happened to mention to us how nice it would be to have us move in with them. Life would be easier for both us and them. They own this beautiful home that's literally on top of a small little Connecticut mountain, that's surrounded by woods. Deer and wild turkey stroll through their yard, it's crazy and beautiful. We decided to leave our home of New York; it felt more like leaving my heart behind but it was the smart thing to do, and moved back to our hometown in Connecticut. We were just forty five minutes outside of the city but it felt so far away. There was no garbage trucks in the middle of the night, no sounds of traffic, it was so quite and dark, there's no street lights on this mountain. All you hear at night is the sound of critters in the woods which to me was scarier than hearing any ruckus outside your door in Brooklyn. This was a good move though and we found this hospital in Wallingford, Connecticut called Gaylord that specialized in spinal cord injuries. I'd even heard that Christopher Reeve had spent some time there awhile back so I figured some additional therapy couldn't hurt. I enjoyed learning as much as I could from different sources. My physical therapist is Ingrid; she's a sweetheart and helps me with my transfers.

Looking back at my discharge paperwork from Mt. Sinai from my initial stay after my accident it said goals to reach for: to feed myself, brush my own teeth and to push my wheelchair independently. It also said that I needed maximum assist with transfers, grooming and dress, which I did at the time. Wow, I couldn't believe I needed that much help. I had just forgotten because I was so busy doing what I had to do to get the job done. I sure have come a long way; still I have yet to begin. My dreams of walking I hold so close to my heart. I would do ANYTHING to reach my goals.

Ingrid shows me this equipment called the F.E.S. Stim Bike which hooks up electrodes to your hamstrings, glutes and quadriceps and fires electrical impulses in a sequential order to stimulate your legs to pedal the bike. From the moment of my first ride I fell in love. Not only does it knock out any spasms for a long while but it helps build muscle mass and fight off atrophy. After a short time Ingrid gets pregnant and we decide to continue on our own, using the Stim Bike alone. It took Jenn once or twice to observe how and where the electrodes go and she had it. I then became a peer counselor talking and helping those who are newly injured. At first it's really emotionally taxing, you're reminded of a time when you were so vulnerable, but this wasn't about me it's about them, most of whom are so appreciative of your visit and their family usually can't thank you enough. In reality it's them I should thank because not so long ago I was in their same position, but with the love and support of my wife and my tenacious desire I realize how far I've come. When rolling up to them, the first thing I tell them is "I'm not gonna lie to you, this sucks. I'm not going to blow sunshine up your butt and tell you everything is going to be alright. What I am going to tell you is that your life is forever changed and this is not the end but it is just the beginning. The best advice I can give is to get out of bed and sit in your chair as long as you can, build endurance, work hard in therapy and adapt to your situation as soon as possible. Your disability does not dictate who you are. You are still the same person. Be mentally strong. You will have good days and bad days but just keep going".

Some kind woman donated a Stim Bike to our local Y.M.C.A. so our days at Gaylord came to an end, which wasn't so bad, instead of a forty minute commute it's only five minutes away and I have accumulated so much workout equipment at home. I have more than I could ask for. We just miss all the people there.

For the next year my energy was focused on researching clinical human trials to repair or restore spinal cord injuries. The United States are so caught up in the bureaucracy of embryonic stem cells vs. adult stem cells. Human trials are not available in the US but my research has shown me that other countries are using stem cells and are having human trials using different techniques.

Now on the subject of adult stem cells having the same possibility as an embryonic stem cell I must admit I am a pro. It's not only because I've done much research on the subject, but I'm also a willing participant in an adult stem cell procedure. It all started when we learned of the Detroit Medical Institute and specifically the Center for Spinal Cord Injury Recovery. They were working on all kinds of people, newly injured, those that had been injured awhile, and those that had adult stem cell surgeries overseas and were doing rehab there. We took a drive out there and were blown away at the facility there. It was beautiful and had equipment I had never seen or could even imagine. I also learned of Dr. Lima who was conducting olfactory stem cell transplantation surgeries in Lisbon, Portugal. He had been a regular surgeon who started working with spinal cord injuries on mice some twenty years ago. He found that the tissues that reside deep in the nasal cavity (olfactory) in humans have the ability to fully regenerate after being totally destroyed. He would remove and then cultivate these cells and apply these tissues at the point of injury in the spinal cord. These cells would provide new nerve signals to bridge the gap at the initial injury site and after time and practice has found significant improvement in patient's ability to walk. He started human trials in 2002 and had a fairly strict set of criteria so that he wasn't just working on individuals for the sake of it, he genuinely cares for his work, his patients and his staff. I can say this personally because I was chosen to be one of his patients, me.... I was so excited; I've always wanted to be a 'space monkey' to take a trip not many have traveled before to an unknown frontier.

The only problem was that it was forty thousand dollars for the procedure alone, and we sure as hell didn't have that kind of money lying around. This is where it pays off living in a small town, because I am half Portuguese, and I was getting my procedure done in Portugal. The local paper caught wind of our story and did a few articles of our story, beautifully reported by a woman named Marietta. She is so kind and did our piece in hopes of us raising enough money; her articles were both well informed and full of hope. Donations came flooding in the mail. We were astonished at the generosities from complete strangers. What killed us the most wasn't the check for a couple of hundred dollars, it was the check for twenty bucks with a note attached that says: "this is all we can afford but your article touched us, good luck and hope you walk again". Such love among strangers makes you almost cry, there's *hope* for us still, and that's still nothing compared to what happened next. Jenn, being the woman that she is, had organized a booklet containing every bit of information about the procedure. A local Portuguese radio news station had read our article and asked us to pay them a visit on their Sunday morning show; we were shocked and of course agreed. The show was run by this charismatic man named Joe who told our story and asked for donations from the listeners. We gave our address and figured that was it, but people started coming to the radio station to give their money right then and there. So many came that a line began to form and then some wanted to introduce themselves, we were so touched and honored at the same time, it was one of the most beautiful displays of human generosity I have ever seen, if not the most. The Masonic Temple of Bethel also helped by having a spaghetti dinner. George was in charge and the members of the temple ran the event. It was a huge success. Thanks to their generosity we were able to come up with the rest of the money for the surgery as well as two months of rehab in Detroit, I was now grateful for living back home, we would have never been able to raise that money while living in the city.

THE SIMPLICITY OF LIFE

The date is set, December 9th, 2005, Lisbon, Portugal. My father grew up in Cascais, Portugal not more than a half hour away; in fact my grandmother still lives there. Going to another country for the first time for something as serious as having major surgery I seriously underestimated. I was just grateful that Jenn and my brother Joe were there with me, for me. The language barrier alone was a major obstacle, there were only two nurses who spoke English in the entire hospital, which was over a hundred years old, in fact most of the buildings in the area were so old, it was quite beautiful. I met Dr. Lima, and having met my share of doctors they tend to be very busy people with only an allotted amount of time for you, the patient, and I'm usually left with questions that are not answered. This wasn't the case with Dr. Lima who, not only spoke fluent English but met with me days before my surgery and spent as much time as I needed and answered every question, he certainly comforted me.

The day came and already having endured everything I had for the last five years, from my initial accident to all the hard work in therapy I figured that this would be a cake walk. I was sadly mistaken. I remember waking up from my surgery and I felt like I had gotten run over by a truck, I could barely speak; I just wanted to see Jenn. They told me that I would be able to but that I needed to get cleaned up first and then I noticed two younger nurses, I kid you not, and they gave me a bed bath. I couldn't wait to tell Jenn who had good laugh. I think she felt bad for me and a sponge bath wasn't going to make her jealous. My brother on the other hand, he was jealous wishing he could get a bath from the two young nurses, he was funny, I'm sure glad he came. I remember feeling like my head was about to fall off the first day or two, and all I kept thinking about was the flight back home which was a nine hour trip. I kept thinking 'I got to get myself strong' and Dr. Lima and the nursing staff kept telling me to 'relax, heal'. I understood their wisdom I'm just too stubborn for my own good and getting back into my wheelchair was priority number one. Now me and Jenn were never the type of people to wait around for permission to do something, anything. If you want to do something, just do it and if someone in authority tells you to stop well then you stop, but I'm not going to wait around and get permission to get in *my* chair so we did. The first time I got into my chair I was all over the place, I couldn't keep my balance and the nurses weren't too pleased but they couldn't speak English so we played it off. I had only a couple of days left before leaving and my strength was slowly returning. I wanted to test my endurance and one day I asked the nurse on duty if I could go out for awhile, she reluctantly agreed and I set my destination to go visit Lady Fatima which is a holy sanctuary. I'm not a religious man but not going to Fatima while in Portugal is like going to Egypt and not taking in the pyramids. My brother had rented a car and drove. He knew how to get there. I didn't realize that it was a two hour trip and once there I couldn't believe how enormous it was. It was so peaceful and serene we could've stayed there all day. Jenn took her pictures with her Kermit the Frog (she never left town without him) which some looked at her with a blasphemous stare. To her Kermit was not a stuffed toy but an actual member of the family, she's had him since she was a kid and has pictures of him from literally every trip they've made together. Why would this not be the same, that's the way she saw it. Jenn's an artist, a real artist not 'artistic', she sees life through a unique set of eyes and I love it. She sometimes does things that I wouldn't necessarily do but I respect her and fell in love because of the way she is. Who am I to change that? I laugh and let her do what she has to do, at Lady Fatima's, without saying a word, she just quietly goes about her business never disturbing anyone. Time went by so quickly, there's so much to take in, and we found ourselves way late so we quickly left, only to run into rush hour traffic. We were so in trouble. When we finally arrived back at the Hopital Egas Muniz we had already missed dinner by over an hour and we tried to sneak back into our room, and yes of course Jenn had converted two chairs into a bed and slept every night with me in my room. The night time nurse came quickly in and through broken English told us that the nurse on duty that allowed us to leave got in trouble from Dr. Lima himself. He wasn't pleased that we were gone for so long. The next day, when he came for his visit I apologized over and over again, and laughed when I told him where we had gone. He said: "why do all Americans want to go to Fatima?" He is a cool doctor. He spent as much time as I needed the day before leaving and he still calls me to this day to check on me from time to time. I've never had a doctor like that. To be honest I was ready to come home. America's stupid little thing's like television, music and food were calling me.

I was told to rest for one month and then start rehab in Detroit. It felt great to be back in my bed and watch a movie and just relax. I knew the hard part was coming. Christmas came up quick and Jenn of course got all of the shopping, and cards done and I was full of the Christmas cheer and *hope*. My resolve and dedication was always strong and never waivered, but this was a real opportunity, it was hope and that's all I ever wanted. I never believed this to be true: that I would never walk again. Never is a long time, without end really in definition and I have to believe some how, some way, some time there will be a cure, I have to or else I will wither and die and there are way too many people I will negatively affect and I can't do that, not me. We watched the movie The Polar Express (great movie) and the whole theme was 'if you believe in Santa Claus than you'll see him'. I took it to heart and realized that if I were to give it a real go and work as hard as I possibly can in Detroit, then I would have to first believe I can walk.

It's January 5th 2006, a new year full of possibilities and we arrive at the Detroit Medical Institute. We're psyched because our apartment suite is beautiful, it's one of the new ones that had just been renovated and it's within walking/wheeling distance to the rehabilitation center, we luck out. I get my schedule and they let me use some of the exercise equipment on our own. Everyone is so nice and it's like a sanctuary, everyone has one goal which is to get you up and walking. We meet so many people who either live in Michigan or are staying at the apartments and mostly everyone is friendly, in fact it seemed like we were getting invited to something almost every weekend. I mostly wanted to stay at home and rest. I was working out like a madman, every day a few hours a day. I figured I was there on a mission and I was going to give it my all, which I did to a fault. They worked me to death too; just standing in leg braces at the parallel bars for five to ten minutes at a time was exhausting. I was working on trunk/torso control, a person with a T8 injury or lower has limited trunk control, so that is usually a starting point for most new *clients*, as they called us. I always needed a nap after each session, it hurt so good. During my stay there I made some cool friends, and met Mike Utley (former Detroit Lions football player who had a spinal cord injury on the field). When I first had my injury and went home, I looked up Mike Utley's 'Thumbs up' website and emailed him and to my surprise he emailed me back with his quick response and up beat attitude. Meeting him was another thing, I am a big football fan and I was kind of star struck. He spent some time talking to me and I told him that I had just had the olfactory tissue procedure done. He was so encouraging, told me about himself and that he was able to gain some return from a neurosurgeon using his specialized biofeedback technique named after him called The Brucker Method which is located in Miami. He then looked at Jenn and said: "what are you feeding him, he needs some meat on his bones" and laughed. Now I will admit that I was a little skinny, I did just have surgery for gods sake, but he was absolutely huge. He was taller than his wife who was standing next to him while he is in his wheelchair. Seriously, I'm so appreciative of our meeting and his advice I will never forget it.

This years Super Bowl, XL is in Detroit on February 5th at Ford Field, again we were psyched because that's about ten blocks away. We didn't know where to go but we were going to go somewhere, it's not every day the Super Bowl is in town. We decide to spend it in a nearby casino where there were tons of Pittsburgh Steelers fans. There were lots of T.V.'s and I park myself in front of the biggest one I can find where individuals wont get in your field of view and I'm in heaven, Jenn's at a nickel slot somewhere and stops by from time to time. This is one of the best Super Bowl parties I've ever been to, mostly everyone in the place was screaming: "one for the thumb, and do it for Jerome"! It was awesome, I'm a Giants fan and I was still rooting for the Steelers.

My time in Detroit was cut short when I started getting severe leg spasms in my left leg only. Wasn't quite sure why, maybe I strained or pulled a muscle, but something definitely wasn't right because I could no longer even stand up in my leg braces, my spasms would knock me right down. So off to home we go again, not feeling defeated because I wasn't walking, it simply 'is what it is' and I had some return in my trunk, right triceps and some chest. I also had the information about biofeedback from Mike Utley and once I got home and got some R and R it would be my next outing. Jenn found out that there were many biofeedback facilities but the one closest to us that taught the Brucker Method was one in Pennsylvania. We scheduled a time when Dr. Brucker himself was going to attend the facility and was going to give a speech concerning his work. We first met Sondra who is a warm and inviting soul, soft spoken and genuine. She is the one who is certified to perform the biofeedback tests, which basically is hooking up electrodes to paralyzed or partially paralyzed muscle groups and are connected to a monitor that displays your nerve signal, which looks like an EKG heart monitor that you see in the hospital. You're given a horizontal line above your average signal which is your potential line and by watching the screen you try and move that signal, the nerve signal to your muscle group, above your given line. It's a totally different way of exercising, instead of using weights to move your muscles, you use your brain (by you viewing the monitor and watching your signal either raise or lower). It's sort of focusing specifically on the root of the signal instead of the muscle group as a whole. If you succeed in raising that signal on the screen up and over your potential goal, then it's reset and you're given an even greater goal now using resistance. I absolutely loved this new way of attempting to gain return, it's like cerebral exercising.

Dr. Brucker showed up and was exactly what you'd think a neuro doctor would look and act like. He is a brilliant man and is passionate about his work and during his lecture I get lost a little because he rarely uses laymen terms. One point he does get across is that doctors just don't know enough about nerves and their behavior, especially in the spinal cord. That doctors are too quick to give a 'you'll never walk again' speech when they are just doctors, not specialist in spinal cord injury and a patient could still regain some function to their paralyzed body. They'll never try because they don't know, unless it's through word of mouth like Mike to me. It's also wonderful to see doctors, like Dr. Lima and everyone in Detroit, who are involved in spinal cord injury recovery, not the most popular of sciences. These doctors and therapist are in it for the sake of helping their fellow man now and for the future, to give hope to those that have none. I'm sure at one point in their early career they could have chosen a different, easier and more conventional direction, but instead chose to follow an unpopular, tougher course. I can't express my eternal appreciation for these individuals that we've met, as well as all of those that are involved with spinal cord injury recovery.

I guess I could go on and on with the "Beyond" part in this chapter so I will sum it up like this. My work with Sondra is on going and encouraging. Through this 'accident'(I've read on a few occasions that there's no such thing as an accident, that it's only ignorance that views it that way) we've done so much, gone so many places and met so many people that seven years earlier I could have never imagined. Dr. Larry Stern, a holistic chiropractor in Bedford Hills, NY is a true and dear friend, one of few individuals who I can have a deep and meaningful conversation. He does some incredible work through NSA. He got me to be able to wiggle my right toes. Then there's Dr. Wise Young from Rutgers University, who is a pioneer in the field of spinal cord injury recovery. He is, as his name indicates, wise yet humble and incredibly approachable as we've attended many of his seminars and he still remembers my name. Another very cool doctor that's in it for the love of man not for personal gain. We've gone to the White House in hopes of helping Bill H.R.810 become a law. It was the coolest thing seeing so many wheelchairs at the hotel we stayed at. We owned it for the two days we were there, able bodied people genuinely looked scared and stepped aside as a train of wheelchairs go flying by. I of course brought my power chair and Jenn her skates and everyone was jealous because we would fly around the city so quickly. At the capital we were honored to meet Dana Reeve, who took the time to talk to many of us individuals. I told her of how Christopher had inspired me when I was in the hospital. What impressed me most was how she listened to me. We were outside and she knelt down beside me, she understood that being a quadriplegic my diaphragm is partially paralyzed which means no strong sneezes, no deep coughs and that it's difficult to project your voice especially if your outside and your talking to someone whose standing over you. You usually get "what, what's that" a lot, but not Dana, she was a pro and as sweet as any person I've ever met. It was a real honor to meet her. We also met Hillary Clinton at that same event, who was a very busy woman, but we were very appreciative to have her there, she is a very passionate woman. Too bad our 'Commander in Chief' has no empathy or foresight and to him everything is a pissing contest and used his very first veto on 7/28/06 to dash the hopes and dreams of our future. All he really did was to delay the inevitable, in my opinion. The needs of the many outweigh the few; it's just a matter of time. As history has shown, man is usually slow in accepting a new science, but eventually he does, he has no choice but to accept its truth. That stubborn asshole just wasted us at least eight good years and like my friend the dog, I just want to scratch an itch with my own fingers. Holding Jenn's hand would be nice too, maybe touch her face, build a sand castle together, shoot a game of pool, or play my Playstation again. God I miss using my hands. Hell I'd settle for using the bathroom by myself. Now that is the *simplicity* I crave.

I guess to sum it all up I feel as though I have been stuck in a repetitive cycle of feeling entrapped in one situation after another my entire life, stemming from my childhood. I could never accept a way of life without choice. Being paralyzed leaves me without choice. I chose, as Christopher Reeve chose, to go forward. I still am a husband and have responsibilities to my wife as well as to my family and friends but I can't choose to walk or not walk. Since most of our adult personality is a product of our childhood, we have the opportunity to learn from previous situations and decisions. I've learned to fight and never accept a way of life that I didn't want. Paralysis will not own me, I will not give in, I can't, and I won't. I can not accept that this is how I will live out the remainder of my days. No! Not even paralysis will own me, tell me how to live. I've always loved a challenge, loved to problem solve. I've always figured a way out of a situation that I didn't want to be in, no matter what it was or how difficult it may be, whether physical or emotional. I've never given up, and I'm not speaking from my ego's point of view, it's just my spirit, which has nothing to do with my mind. I still am that little boy in that race who thought he was going to lose, until that special reserve kicked in and won me that race.

Chapter Four

HAND ENVY

Jenn calls it hand envy, but it's not envy that I'm feeling, it's more like admiration. You see at certain times, it could be at any given moment, I find myself just flat out staring at a person in real life, like at the gym or an actor in a movie who's usually doing some kind of strenuous physical activity. It's not necessarily the individual that captivates my attention, it's usually the body or even the body part, like the muscles in a well developed arm or how incredible the human hand works. The human hand has twenty seven bones and numerous muscles and tendons that have to be subdivided into two groups. To me that's amazing. They all work together to make the hand strong enough to manipulate strong, heavy objects and yet have the amazing fine motor skills able to thread a needle. Forget about the forearms, biceps and triceps, I'm just as fascinated with these muscle groups. Before I was injured when I worked out, I just worked on a group of muscles one day, another group the next day (back and bi's Monday, chest and tri's Wednesday etc.). I never gave much thought as to how each muscle worked; its purpose or its function. Why would I? Now here I am with ability to control just my biceps (the pull muscle), but without the use of my triceps (the push muscle), half of the forearm muscles and of course no hand function. Trying to fight off atrophy I work on these muscles, hoping to regain strength and function, which I have seen some progress. So when staring it's more like studying the body and then envisioning my arm the same. Even walking is incredible. To the able bodied person this activity is an unconscious act, but if you think about the mechanics and balance that is involved in walking, the number of bones, muscles, nerves, ligaments and tendons all working in unison. It's incredible. On occasion, we go to Atlantic City, with my in laws, and a favorite past time of ours is sitting on the boardwalk and 'people watching'. We always have a blast making observations to the myriads of visitors as they pass by, our guilty pleasure. I usually take this opportunity to really observe the motions of walking, putting it in my memory banks so that one day I'll use this same strategy when I begin my first stages of returning to the upright world. I make no mistake about it; I thoroughly understand how difficult walking will be. I've stood up with braces on my legs at the parallel bars in rehab at the Hospital for Rehabilitation in Detroit, and just standing for minutes at a time is extremely exhausting. It's incredible how many muscles that are involved in simply just standing up. I

HAND ENVY

once heard a definition of walking as: a series of controlled falls. I thought that was brilliant. I could 'people watch' all day.

    I drive Jenn crazy at times when we're watching a movie together. For example we were watching an action flick with Brad Pitt who was pointing his gun with intensity throughout the entire movie. Now to me Brad Pitt has got the picture perfect arms for a man, they are perfectly defined. That's usually when I press pause on the remote and am like: "man do you see his forearms?" or if we're watching a magician as he uses 'slight of hand' to perform a trick, like my favorite trick, when he manipulates a coin across his hand using just his fingers. His fingers have such dexterity that they almost have a life of themselves, it's truly hypnotic. Then Jenn usually tries to grab the remote from me. She understands that I'll probably do this another couple of times throughout the movie.....honestly sometimes I don't know how she puts up with my manic behavior. It's just that I have such an appreciation of the body's physical function so much now then I ever have before. It's not envy, its admiration. That's my story and I'm sticking to it.

THE SIMPLICITY OF LIFE

Chapter Five

DRIVER & PASSENGER

I look at life now through eyes of one who understands his mortality and how fragile life can really be. Before my injury I never took into account that I could seriously get hurt or injure someone else while I was driving. Statistically males from the age of eighteen to thirty are more inclined to have spinal cord injuries and are from automobile accidents. I now realize that there are two kinds of people in this world, those who are drivers and those who are passengers. The drivers feel as though they are in complete control of their vehicle on the road and their own lives as well as their passengers. Often they tend to be occupied with getting to their destination, focused only on getting from point A to point B in as quick and efficient manner as possible. Which is not necessarily a bad thing, these people like getting things done. Then there are the passengers like me. These people are the ones that watch the surroundings go by, without themselves being in control. They trust the driver (more or less), maybe play the occasional co-pilot, helping out, play with the radio or watch the people in their cars drive by. I wonder where they are going. Why are they in such a rush? Is it really that important? Do they even understand how fragile life could be at any given moment, just because up to this moment in their lives they have escaped an accident, maybe even a tragic one? No they don't. They go about driving as though nothing can ever happen, even though they increase their chances immensely by their irrational driving behavior. Selfish, that's it in a nutshell. Now I'm not talking about aggressive driving, I'm talking about those idiots who fly down the slow lane only to cut back right in front of you at the last second, as if jumping ahead of a couple of cars is really going to save that much time. There's the driver who drives exclusively in the fast lane at extreme high speed regardless of the time of day. Then there's the oblivious driver who's in the fast lane doing just the speed limit never looking in their rear view mirror, there's a line of cars behind you that's waiting on you. It's this type of driving, in my opinion, that helps create traffic jams in the first place. No regard for you or anyone else. They are the only ones that are important. Unfortunately this is just a reflection of our society. It shouldn't be. The road is like a river and we flow in its path. On a highway there are usually either two or three lanes: slow, medium and fast. The fast lane should be used for passing that's why it's called a 'passing lane'. It's the fool that abuses this lane, which is like a luxury lane if you really think about it. If you're in the medium lane and the driver in front of you is driving too slow you have the option to pass the driver in front of you by using the 'passing lane', it's a fascinating system. On occasion we come across a pack of cars cruising approximately at the same speed. By observing the other people who are around you in your pack, that flow of traffic, you pick and choose what it has given you, your opportunity to pass or let pass. That helps traffic move along smoothly. Then it happens again, the idiot who cuts you off, who believes his or her own life is more important than yours on this road that you both share at this same exact moment in time. This causes you to brake quickly, which causes the person behind you to brake. That is what disturbs the flow of the river. In my observation that is what causes traffic jams (for the most part). I had never realized this, nor was able to observe any of this before my injury because I was always the driver. I always loved to drive, be in control of the situation. I controlled me or my passenger's outcome, the time of arrival from point A to point B and of course I was one of those idiots who thought saving five minutes of my time was THAT important. I thought I was a great driver because I could sneak in front of that car and see five moves ahead of time. I was such an idiot! I had no respect for mine or my passenger's life. I had no idea how precious, valuable and fragile life can be. Not until I became the passenger. I observe life so differently now. I see that baby in the back of that SUV. I see the face of that college girl driving alone, singing at the top of her lungs to her favorite song. They're real people inside these metal boxes. There are real people inside, with real lives and real families. Why did I not see this before? How could I have been so oblivious to this before? I also see the wisdom of Jenn's driving. I kid her about her driving "God you drive like an old lady", now that she was doing all the driving (something I know she hates since she used to make anyone else drive, even her car). I now have my license but the tables have turned and Jenn always bullies me to let her drive. She says I take too long to transfer out of my wheelchair and into the driver's seat which honestly it does take awhile but she can be so rude about it. She'll say 'you're gonna take forever let me drive'. She has never treated me different since my accident and it's always refreshing to hear brutal honesty. She never lets me get away with anything which is a good thing. I see that you don't have to be out in front of the pack, but running with the flow of the river. That's what really matters. It's really the most efficient way to travel, both for yourself, and your fellow human passengers. I must admit that I still think she drives a little too slow though. She makes up for it by speeding up, when she's in the middle lane, to block in the current idiot trying to pass on the right. You should hear her laugh when she's successful at blocking them in, causing them to have to brake, slow down, switch lanes to go back into the passing lane and fly by us as though their lives have just been tragically altered. She just wants to be passed on the correct side. It's seems as if it's the end of the world for these people, who occasionally flip us off, which brings us an even greater laugh. We laugh not because she pissed someone off but because we understand the importance of life and the importance of keeping the river flowing smoothly.

THE SIMPLICITY OF LIFE

Chapter Six

THE BED

My bed has a life of its own. It comforts me. It tells me to relax, "your daily struggling is over, lay back, the pressure, the pain on your butt, legs and back is finally over. Here is where you belong, stress-free. You're out of the way, no one asking if you need help with this or that. No responsibilities, no one staring at you out in public, no problems, no discomfort. Stay here. It's safe. You can have your remote and T.V., your blanket and if you need anything, anything at all, food, medicine, drink, you need not struggle, your wife is right there, as she always has been, to get you everything you need. Life's tough enough, you deserve to relax, haven't you been through enough already!" What it doesn't tell me is that it makes me LAAAZY! God I could stay in bed forever. I forget the old saying, "If you don't use it, you loose it." I'm not quite sure where or when it reared its ugly head, my obsession with being a perfectionist. It's almost out of control at times, never really being happy with my accomplishments, trying harder or better even at the most simplest, stupid things. It usually takes Jenn or another individual to point out my manic behavior before I realize what I'm doing. I've always considered this character trait of mine a 'GOOD THING'. So naturally after I had my accident, well maybe 6 months after, I figured that life had prepared me for this task at hand: rehabilitation. If I didn't walk out of the hospital, then I would dedicate my life to getting it back. I work out for hours a day, at least 5 days a week, working on each muscle group, strengthening those that I have and using electrical stim to those that are paralyzed to promote muscle growth and hopes of nerve signal regeneration, just enough to increase my level of independence. Using my standing frame, which is a rehabilitation device that when secured in allows you to literally stand up bearing weight on your hips, ankles and feet, and using the F.E.S. bike all in an effort to keep strong, maintain blood pressure, and resist atrophy. I don't even realize how hard I work. I just want to regain the use of my body again. I have seen a lot of progress but I still can't use my hands or walk. I can't give up and then it hits me... depression. Some would even call it reality. "Give it up, your paralyzed, your not gonna get better, your in denial, deal with it!" That's when it calls me: my bed. It tells me to stop and relax. Evil thoughts begin to creep in, slowly at first, and then there I am contemplating the details to my suicide. How can live the rest of my life trapped in this broken

THE BED

body that I have to drag around. If I were an animal they would have put me down long ago. How can I do this to Jenn, enslave her to this life, I know that she would never leave. We'll never do the things that we used to do before I got hurt and don't give me the bullshit 'if you did it before you can do it again' because that only fly's for most paraplegics (who have the use of their hands). Me, I'm a quadriplegic, no hands, triceps, and limited trunk control, whatever I do is going to take much effort, but honestly I'm pretty strong for a C5-C6 quad, a lot are in power chairs (not electric chairs, which put people to death) but this is me, I'll never touch her the same, never make love the same. Can I cope? Sure, but not to sound melodramatic, it feels like I've been coping my whole life. There's no hope for a cure because of our stubborn, dumb ass, ignorant, unintelligent dictator George W. Fucking Bush. I feel like an old man waiting for the grim reaper. I'm trapped inside this body, trapped in this bed. I don't know how long I can keep this up; I don't know how long I can keep doing this to my wife. Do I stay here and allow Jenn to take care of me, never really living, never having children (not that I wasn't able to but how can I burden her with so much responsibility to care for both of us), my mind shackled to this thing, this body that at one time used to make her feel safe, that was once her protector, her man. If I really loved her I'd set her free, maybe check myself into a home and then take care of business. God knows I have enough sleeping pills and muscle relaxers to get the job done. Some others might live their lives like this but not me; I'm not supposed to live out my life like this, not me. I so don't fear death or its ramifications; at least I won't be trapped here like this. That damn bed. Keeps me unmotivated. Keeps me depressed. It pollutes my brain. It drains my energy. At the same time it's my safe haven, it's my comfort place. It's so crazy, this ride. I go out for dinner with my wife, we laugh, we kiss, and I look into her beautiful eyes and I say, "How can I ever leave her alone, as much as she's done for me, how faithful she is, how much it would crush her, the pain would stay with her for the rest of her life." Jenn has been my biggest fan. Since day one she believes I would walk again, that this did happen for a reason. She says she doesn't care about my disability. She needs me, her husband. My bed tells me, "If you really love her you'll let her go. She'll move on eventually and maybe meet someone and have children since you won't be the one you idiot. You just had to dive in that goddamn pool. Now look at you…your road kill at best. Do you really want to hold her down, she's an independent woman and she can do anything, anything, besides wasting precious time of her life taking care of this old man."

It feels like a catch 22 sometimes while I'm lying there. I should be grateful that such a wonderful woman would stick through it all, not only emotionally, but physically being my caregiver. Any man in my position would do anything to be with such a woman. At the same time how could I do this to this woman that I love so much, and who loves me back just the same. That damn bed! I have to stay active, stay strong, and believe, not just for myself but for my wife. We both deserve that. I will do it. People say all the time, usually in reference to their

THE BED

career, 'If you believe it, it will happen for you.' That's so easy to say but to do it is another, especially this, the impossible, to regain life in this lifeless body. I wish it was as easy as just pursuing a career. I do believe (depending on the day) that my life was destined for this challenge, and that, through patience, time, dedication and hard work, while trusting in my intuition, that this latest test will reveal a person in me that I previously would have never known. I'll be that special person that I've always believed I am. I have a plan; it's just believing in that plan, executing that plan, and then owning that plan. It has become a personal credence of mine for just about every aspect of my life. Whether it be a project that requires my physical involvement, or working on my personal flaws as a person. 1. First recognize it. Confront it. Stare at it right in its face, despite what your ego tries to convince you of otherwise. 2. Work on it, correcting this flaw, slowly at first, understanding when and why you act or react the way you do, when you do. Never winning this battle, just a continuous fight. One step forward, two steps back. The key to this step is patience, and determination that one day you won't have this weakness, this flaw (usually created by our unconscious mind by some kind of insecurity, usually from our childhood that was never addressed. I think I've read too much Jung). 3. Owning it. Sometimes it could take years to finally overcome some flaw, but one day you will. Maybe you won't even realize you have until something reminds you of something else and you realize that you would have reacted or said something in a totally different way, the old way, the more immature way. Then you laugh because you see how you've grown, without really even knowing it. Isn't that instinctively one of our purposes in life, besides the obvious need to procreate and pass on our seed? The need to improve on ourselves, grow, become a better human being, not the pursuit to have the best job, nicest car, you know, the ones the neighbors could see and think, "I must be doing o.k. for myself". Let us not forget about the two children per American household and owning your own home with the white picket fence. When we are done multi-tasking these simple tasks of our lives that society has dictated for us and have accomplished all of this by our middle ages, we have successfully avoided the most important accomplishment of life: understanding ourselves. Understanding who we really are and why we do the things we do and then trying to evolve to a better, higher self. I would have never seen or understood this in its entirety unless my life came to a screeching halt, because my physical body and my daily activities were slowed down, I began to see life a little slower, more simple. Suddenly complaining about having to go to work, even though I was tired and wasn't in the mood to do it, seemed so ridiculous. That was the one thing I remember hearing the most after coming home from the hospital. How much people love to complain about their lives. "What the hell could be so hard, so miserable in your life and why are you sharing this with me". Shit I used to even complain how miserable my life was. God how wrong I was. I failed to realize how simple life is. If you don't like something about your life, just change it. It's really just that simple. Just follow those three golden rules. Of course I would never have realized this had I have to see life a little slower now these days. In

THE BED

this way I feel grateful for this accident. One day I feel as though I will return to an able body life but I will forever live a disabled life in my heart. I just gotta stay away from that goddamn bed!

THE SIMPLICITY OF LIFE

Chapter Seven

JENN

............and so I've saved the best for last.

What can I say? How can I possibly put into written word the one who is known as Jennifer Rick Stagl Fernandes. She is so complex with so many different facets to her personality, she fits into no individual category. In the days before I started writing this chapter I felt very different. The previous chapters just flowed through me like a river; I never had to think about it, words just came. Afterwards I realized that I was negligent in describing in detail my best friend and her impact on me and my life. But to describe who she is, individually, as her own person and also as my wife, this was all together something different. How she is and how I perceive her to be, both before and after my injury. She is more than a profile of her likes and dislikes, her physical features and her personal accomplishments. It's like photo copying a multi-facet diamond; the picture doesn't do it justice.

I guess I could simply start from the beginning. It was my brother Joe who I will always be grateful for by making our paths cross. I was 21, and was on workmen's comp and decided to take the summer off. Sit back, drink some beers with my brother and a handful of friends, I was having a blast. Joe was working a couple of jobs and one was at a local entertainment complex. Roller skating was pretty much the only qualification for the job, and since I was a kid I loved skating. So instead of returning to my job in Greenwich, which I loved but the commute killed me, I chose the fun local job instead, really it was fate that was calling me. Compared to my last job, this one was a piece of cake. It was my first day. I was a skate guard for the roller rink section, complete with the referee t-shirt and whistle. It was a Saturday afternoon and the rink was packed with kids. I whipped around that rink as fast as I could, I missed skating. I was 9 years old all over again. And then she showed up with her referee shirt and whistle. She had short spiky red hair and big John Lennon eye glasses and immediately yelled at me to slow down. "Me, she told me to slow down. That's my job to tell others that, not have someone tell me to. I had the shirt". Who was this girl? Why is she here? Does this rink really need two people or is she checking up on me? Look at her, just standing there like a cop, waiting to arrest someone. She has her own nice set of custom skates, while I'm here sporting rentals. I'm a little embarrassed. I skated off the rink and again she skates over to me and shouts: "You gotta stay on the floor for the shift". I couldn't believe this shit! What a bitch. Why did she have it in for me? So I stayed and waited... for my turn. Then it happened, she skated off the floor. I skated quickly up to her quickly and yelled "Hey, I thought we were supposed to stay on the floor". She gave me a dirty look and we skated back onto the skate floor. I got her back. That was my introduction to Jenn Ellis.

Jenn was the complete opposite of any girl than I had ever simply known, forget about dating. Thinking back, I remember thinking: "why does everyone who works here want to know what she's doing after work"? This job was like a little fraternity, mostly everyone were good friends and hung out after work, drink some beers and do some kind of activity. It was always Jenn who everyone looked to for what they were going to do that night. She was like the ring leader and everyone was happy to just be a part of it. I didn't get it. Being new I hardly knew anyone, except Joe, and when he didn't work my shift I was alone. I didn't mind not fitting in, I had enough drama going on in my personal life, but I sure did want to hang out after work. It wasn't until one night after work, I was about to get in my car and some of the guys started throwing a football around in the parking lot, and then it happened. I saw Jenn launch that football with a tight spiral at least 60 yards, the length of the parking lot, and my perspective of her shifted in the blink of an eye. She overthrew the guys catching it and the ball landed near me, so I ran over, picked it up and launched it back to her and just like that I was sworn in.

In the following days and weeks that followed, it was always Jenn who composed the night's events. Whether it was playing midnight basketball, poker on the floor in the parking lot (Jenn was of course always the dealer) or going on a scavenger hunt through town. Her cars trunk was full with baseballs and a wiffle ball bat, a basketball and various footballs, all different sizes and types. Who was this girl? She had just graduated from Art College and had her own thing going on, not just drifting along waiting for something to happen. She's a leader, bold and never afraid to speak her mind. She's an artist, not artistic but a really for real artist, one who denies her existence but her work proves her true. I had never really interacted with her directly, there was always so many people around and she was always surrounded by the hanger on's. Besides more often than not Joe was there, and oddly enough he knew Jenn from the old days when we were kids and used to go roller skating at that same place. The face of the building and most of the inside was now totally different but not that rink, that rink was still the same. God I used to love to race around on the far outside as fast as I could, what a rush just gliding along the floor, I felt so free. Joe being two and a half years older than me hung out with the cool kids in the middle of the rink showing off their skating abilities. Don't ask me how but Joe had somehow scammed his way to owning his own pair of skates leaving me to use the rentals. I was a nerd from the beginning. I just liked to skate fast. Joe on the other hand had skills and that's what you need for admittance to the center circle, customized personal skates and skills. Guess who just so happened to be there with her

JENN

cool skates and moves, Jenn, who of course ruled the circle. So Joe and Jenn's friendship had begun some ten years ago and now reacquainted he introduced me to Jenn that night and we talked and talked and talked some more.

The moment that transcended that and transformed both of our lives was the 'catfish' night. There was this lake that a bunch of us would go to after work and hang out at the beach. This night we sat on the brick wall passing different bottles of Boones Farm wine among each other. Jenn takes her shoes and socks off, and jumps into the sand and laughing like a school girl begins to build a sand castle. She is completely covered in sand and without a care in the world; she looks like she's having the time of her life. Everyone is getting a kick watching her. I watch her and she looks like she's having so much fun. Who cares if you get dirty or what it may look like from others, she's having a blast. I instinctively jump down and join her digging in the sand. We start by making the moat and then build the base. We immediately work together as if we'd done this a hundred times before. When digging, we come across this huge rock and we dig feverishly at it until we uncover it. It takes the both of us to pick it up and we run to the water as if to return it to its rightful place. We throw it in and it makes a giant splash and we both, on a synchronized, unconscious wavelength yell out: "CATFISH", as if we had just freed it from its entombment. I can't say for sure whether any one of us had ever yelled out 'catfish' whenever a fish jumped out of the water as we sat on that wall so many nights before, but there was a type of kindred bond that was born when we synchronized our emotions aloud with a simple word: **Catfish**. After that night, not a day went by that we didn't see each other.

I remember talking, just talking, for hours. After our motley crew had ended its night, we always met up and just hung out, doing nothing but talking. Time seemed to both stand still and yet fly by so quickly. Sometimes in her car in the parking lot, other times in mine, we talked about life. We were just getting to know each other. Jenn is a person that just makes things happen, if you want something, just go and do it. She never sees the obstacles just the outcome. I remember confiding in her one late night that I secretly always wanted to be an actor and to my amazement she said that was cool and that I should go to school for it. I was expecting the 'you're crazy' response that I usually got when I rarely expressed my secret to a friend. Living in small town Danbury, Connecticut, becoming a successful actor is like climbing Mt. Everest. To Jenn it is simply started by attending college. Who is this girl? One night we were hanging out playing Tetris on Nintendo, she only likes playing puzzle type video games, and I looked over at her and I remember thinking " I really like this girl, she's really cool". Before that I had never thought of Jenn in that way, we had never flirted, we had just become friends, good friends. She was so much fun to hang out with. Most girls just crowded my space after awhile. It was never like that with her. It felt like I was on my surfboard riding a wave and Jenn was riding with me on her own board on her own wave. I never felt crowded. It never felt like she was in my personal space, she always had her own thing going, we just were sharing time and space together and it was effortless. Shortly after that *it happened*. Looking back now it seems so corny and typical but at the time it was spontaneous and felt just right. We were hanging out after work in the back of our job, a bunch of us. We had gotten in trouble by management for hanging out in the parking lot so we moved our party to the back of the building. It was a beautiful cloudless starry night. I was looking at the constellations and was pointing one out to Jenn. I leaned in, and grabbed her hand to help guide her as we pointed to the big dipper. I swear I never planned it, I just felt compelled and I kissed her, nothing sloppy, just a soft sweet kiss. It felt so right.

The next day we met up before work to get something to eat, our first date. We agreed to meet at the local hotdog stand nearby work and I remember being so hung over that I couldn't even eat, I just wanted to see her. Jenn ordered three hotdogs with sauerkraut, catsup and mustard and had no problem eating them. It was awesome watching a girl be real and not be afraid of who she was. I just couldn't believe such a little girl could eat so much.

She moved in shortly there after. Me, Joe and Jenn all living under one roof, it was one party after the next. It was the best time of my life. With her it always was and always will be a battle of wits, in a good way. She's always challenged me knowing I would never back down from anything. It was a good practice as time would later tell. I always gave it back, we both hate to lose at anything, whether we're playing checkers or trying to be the first to find the hidden items in a picture from a Highlights magazine. She was my best friend and one of the guys, there wasn't anything I didn't mind doing with her. One night as I mentioned previously, when we were in Manhattan after watching the play Cats, I mention how awesome it would be to live here and she just said "lets do it" and just like that, nine months later, we were both enrolled in the School of Visual Arts and living in the east village. She's magic, just makes things happen. Working, living and going to school together was like nothing, if anything it was comforting. The friends and memories we made that first year could fill a lifetime. Like my boy Tony, who lived in Harlem and showed me what it's like to really be a part of New York and Nathan who is a free spirit that travels and photographs the country through a unique and artistic set of eyes. They were always 'our' friends. We're still friends with them some fourteen years later.

After Jenn finished her degree we moved down south and experienced another side of America. Jenn of course fit right in, even started gaining a southern drawl. Me, not so much. I missed the heartbeat of the city but it was quite the experience. Isn't that life though, a series of experiences and I spent most of them with my best friend. It's been nice growing up with Jenn. It's nice having so many stories that we shared together. We've done so much together and yet we've had our moments where we've been apart. What love story doesn't have its comedy and tragedy; this is what makes for a rich relationship. For a short time we lived apart in different states and yet not more than a day or two go by that we didn't talk. We knew that one day life would bring us back together again. Life's

JENN

been a thrilling roller coaster ride with Jenn. Complete with it's up's and down's, twists and turns, in the end your left winded and exhausted but with a huge smile and you can't wait to get back on line to experience it again.

After seven years we decided that we wanted a baby. Her parents never judged me or gave me a hard time about us living together without being married, since she was the first in her family to do so. To us we could have lived together forever 'in sin' because it was a marriage just without the paper. Her parents, as lenient as they were with us, put their foot down when it comes to bringing a child into this world unwed. I have always respected Bill and Barbarajean. I respect them more than I respect even my own parents. They've always treated me as their own son; they were the family I had always wished for, how could I possibly disappoint them and so on May 15th 1999 Jennifer became my wife. I've already mentioned my breakdown after becoming married, feeling as though I needed to be something that I wasn't. Time just ticked away. Funny thing about time, it waits for no one and when you finally figure something out, you look up and time has swiftly passed by without your knowledge or consent.

One year rapidly goes by and all is right in the world again, everything feels right, just in time for that fateful day of June 17th 2000. After my injury, she never left my side. I remember during one of our first conversations I asked her "What if I can't hold your hand and walk in the park anymore?" Her response was "Then I will sit on your lap and we'll roll". That answer is so Jenn. I knew from her response that we were going to get through this together. After coming home she knew that I couldn't go everywhere with he and my insecurity could play tricks on me and think that she's having an affair. Instead Jenn goes to great measures to let me know where she is at all times just to ease my mind, such selflessness. She harbors no animosity to me for changing the dynamics of our life. She never complains when she throws the garbage out, my job, a man's job. She stays with me; for God's sake she forgoes a life of normalcy to stay with me, to care for me. She says I'm still the same person I was before my injury and so it's easy to live this life. I say if it not for her I wouldn't be the person I am, who've I've become and ultimately who I'll be. People always ask how I'm doing, never asking how she's doing and she never complains. She always has my best interest in mind, even to a fault. She's by far the most selfless person I've ever known. She is forever thinking of others before herself and she doesn't even realize it. She would prefer to play with the kids rather than socialize with the adults at a gathering. She'll forever be that little girl trapped in an adult body. Jenn's the only person I know that can accomplish twenty different tasks in one day and not even be winded. She's so simple; the littlest thing will bring her happiness. She finds more joy in getting a prize from a gumball machine or playing bingo then fancy dinners and expensive jewelry. She always gets what she wants and yet she wants very little. As long as she has her acrylic paints, brushes, crayons, her power tools, her computer with a scanner and printer and her Kermit shoes; she's a happy camper. She is an angel. As many times as people are referred to as angels; this one literally saved my life in more ways than one. She's earned her wings.

THE SIMPLICITY OF LIFE

Chapter Eight

THE GREAT GARBAGE DEBATE

When discussing the topic of embryonic stem cells, I am still astonished at how passionate of an opinion each side has. I would imagine it was something similar to the great debate of Roe verses Wade on Jan 22, 1973, which was concluded by the United States Supreme Court that most laws against abortion violated individuals' constitutional rights to privacy under the Due Process Clause of the Fourth Amendment. Thirty four years later it's still a hot topic and that's what this seemingly feels like, pro choice verses pro life. Thank god our fore fathers had the foresight in writing the Constitution which stands as a model of cooperative statesmanship and the art of compromise. Thomas Jefferson in 1802 was credited with the phrase *separation of church and state* when he referred to the First Amendment as creating a wall of separation between church and state. Now most pro life individuals whose life beliefs are based on the bible or some other religious conviction argue that life begins at conception and those embryos that are grown artificially, through science, are okay with the method but not with the destruction for the use of science. To me that's just hypocritical, besides this way of thinking runs against our own Constitution. It's not that stem cells are the definitive cure all, but they represent so much hope to so many. Every 45 minutes someone has a spinal cord injury in the United States alone. I can only speak on my behalf but if I were disabled with anything besides a spinal cord injury or neurological disorder there would be *some* kind of hope for recovery, instead of 'here's your wheelchair, good luck with the rest of your life'. Honestly it feels like my government has let me down, where are my rights?

This kind of thinking reminds me of the days of the scientist Galileo Galile who championed a heliocentric model of the universe (the center of universe was the sun) which was a controversial subject within his lifetime. The geocentric view (the earth being the center of the universe) had been dominant since the time of Aristotle and Galileo's opposition to this view resulted in his condemnation in 1616 by the Catholic Church as contrary to scripture. Galileo spent the last years of his life under house arrest on orders of the Inquisition. This great man as time would attest to, will later become known as the father of modern science and physics. It wasn't until 1687, seventy one

THE GREAT GARBAGE DEBATE

years later that a published work by Sir Isaac Newton that confirmed his work and toppled the geocentric world view and advancing the scientific revolution. Something so simple as 'the sun being the center of the universe' now a days, was such a hot topic back then. Science prevailed back then as I'm sure it will again in the future, and I'm sure the stem cell debate will be looked upon in the same manner, I just hope it doesn't take as long. I personally don't have any problem with religion, everyone needs something to believe in, it's the dogma that I just can't take.

I don't mean to go into semantics but to put it simply there are 356 Assisted Reproductive Technology (in vitro) laboratories in the U.S. alone. Depending on which poll you read there are approximately 500,000 frozen embryos. Each family donates twenty four ova and sperm, two to four embryos are then implanted into the woman and hopefully at least one of the four will begin its remarkable dance of life. The remaining eighteen to twenty embryos are frozen and await their destiny. If the original procedure fails to produce pregnancy, then some embryos may be thawed out and a second implantation may be attempted. At this point either the couple is pregnant or not, and if not then the odds are against them unfortunately. The remaining five day old embryos have many options as to their out come, the family can continue to pay for their cryogenesis, have them disposed or donate them to another family looking to adopt. They can find a facility and donate them to science where they can be used for stem cells. These cells are pluripotent which means that they have the ability to become any cell, which is incredible and a new frontier. A cell that has the capabilities to become *any* possible cell is revolutionary.

Bill H.R.810 (Stem Cell Research Enhancement Act) is the bill that is asking the government for funding so that science can further research and make cures for paralysis, Parkinson's, diabetes, Alzheimer's and countless other diseases and disabilities a reality. If this bill, which was passed by the senate on July 18, 2006, was not vetoed by our president on July 19, 2006 (the only time in his whole presidency that he chose to use the power to veto), it would allow families that have those remaining embryos that are frozen and that are no longer going to be used, the option to donate to science....for hope, no cloning or anything like that, basically we're just asking that families be allowed to donate what would become a laboratories garbage. Also, there is a difference between adult stem cells, which already has a character and embryonic stem cells, which have the possibilities to become any cell. Like I mentioned before, embryonic stem cells are not proven to cure paralysis in humans yet but they do have the potential and represent hope in a sad point in time.

We are at war, and most of us want out. There seems to be annoyance everywhere, between global warming, rising oil prices, terrorism, our economy, and the immigration issues the future feels dark. Now imagine a world where disorders are a thing of the past. The disabled are able and broken organs can now be fixed anew. I can smell it, what a wonderful world this could be.....one filled with hope. As the years that followed Galileo a revolution was born and the world was never the same. History is filled with many such stories which is why, to me, it's important to look to the past to be able to look to the future.

In reality there is no hot topic debate. Pro life people want to argue over when an embryo is considered a life and that we shouldn't be playing god by destroying frozen embryos. They fail to understand or admit that the remaining eighteen to twenty are going to be destroyed by going in the garbage anyway. Wouldn't it be considered pro life to save lives with those potentially discarded embryos? How can you argue against that!

THE SIMPLICITY OF LIFE

Chapter Nine

EPILOGUE

I've been writing 'Simplicity' one chapter at a time over the past six years, from time to time as the feelings hits, without any discipline. It wasn't until another tragedy that's happened in my life that gave me the focus that I needed, but this one hurt real bad. The first time me and my brother Joe were separated we were very close, but we were just kids, our personalities were still just growing. When we reunited I was twenty years old and he was about twenty three. I still longed for that close bond that we had as children, but we were young adults now and life had taken us in different directions. We were different people now and saw life differently, but our love for each other never changed, it still ran deep. Joe was much more reserved than I am. The moment I was out of my mother's clutches I always felt the need to speak out and say what's on my mind. I never cared if I sounded crazy or not. I just knew that I didn't ever want to suppress any emotion, good or bad, just get it off my chest. Meeting Jenn who has the same personality helped me be me and so I grew even more. Unfortunately Joe never did find his 'Jenn' and usually kept his feelings in check; he would open up on occasion to me and or Jenn. It was because of Joe that I met Jenn and although we both loved the rest of our family, we didn't really respect them, they never earned it. So it was just the two of us still, until life intervened and separated us again but this time it was for good. Joe died March 19th, 2007 at the age of thirty nine alone in his condominium. I was his emergency contact; the one person he trusted the most should anything happen to him. It was me; his little brother that he trusted the most. It was unbelievable how much it hurt, I now know how Jenn felt when less then a year before her big brother Billy had suddenly died. Thank god for Jenn's brothers who helped with all of the arrangements.

Let's just say that on my brother's burial day I still had his keys to his place and everyone wanted to secure his belongings that day. I was so grief struck and I couldn't believe we were having this conversation, give it a couple of days, a week and then we can deal with business. Unfortunately my uncle was going out of town the next day and my father was going on vacation the day after so they were in a hurry to take care of everything, I was shocked......vacation? I couldn't even think straight or eat and everyone was in a hurry to get into his place, I

EPILOGUE

thought how incredibly heartless, shouldn't we be grieving as a family? I refused to give them the keys, my brother did entrust me with them and I had no problem going through his belongings together as a family, I was just sickened that we were even talking about it at the wake. My uncle proceeded to call me a cripple and that I was incapable of handling my brothers business. Silly ignorant man, I may be disabled but there is nothing I am not *able* to do. My uncle had never spoken to me with such disrespect in my thirty seven years of life. I realize what little cohesiveness we had as a family was because of Joe and now that he's gone the family crumbled.

Jenn and her family have always been the family I ever wished for and they grieved with me as a family, supported me and loved me. They hurt too, Joe visited our family every holiday and they had accepted him too as one of the family, not just in name.

I had once read, maybe heard that when someone we know that's dear to us dies, we should be consoled by the fact that they have moved on to a higher existence. That in reality it is our own selfish thoughts that makes *us* sad because they are no longer with *us*, that *we* can no longer have them in *our* lives. Like I'll never get another hug from Joe again, never go to another game with him, never do anything ever again with him. What I do have is tons of pictures of him, (thanks Jenn) I have video of his speech to me and Jenn as my best man in our wedding and his recorded voice to listen to whenever I feel the need to. I also have all of my memories and that's all I can ask for.

THE SIMPLICITY OF LIFE

To be honest, unselfishly I am glad Joe no longer is struggling, paddling upstream constantly. It didn't matter how many times we talked man to man about the simplicity of life, he'd get it but only for a short time. The slave to the grindstone mentality would creep back in and he was back in its grips, worrying, worrying, worrying, but now he's free and I love him. Ironically I was set free too. Joe was the one who always suggested we get together with my father, which to me I could or could not go. Nothing personal to him, he just abandoned me as a child, made no effort to contact me growing up. Even as an adult I had to find him and call him to get together. It always felt hard and after the fiasco with my father and uncle at my brother's wake, I was treated as though I was never a member of their family. I felt relieved to walk/roll away from that part of my family, yet I felt so alone.

As far as my mother is concerned, she was hanging by a thread by me, and I grew tired of her attempts to get me to rejoin the religion. Now when I had to be the one to tell her that her son had died, she screamed with horror and wept uncontrollably only as a mother could, I would imagine. For the first time in years I felt sincere sorrow for her. She immediately lied to me when I asked her if she had heard from my sister because I had to get a hold of her right away. I had not seen her in years. My mother said that she hadn't heard from her in months, wasn't sure if she was still living in Florida and wasn't sure if she had her number but she'd check. Five minutes later my sister called me back from my god fearing mother's apartment.

EPILOGUE

She then, for reasons unknown, doesn't go to her own sons' funeral.

Now I am officially free. The only thing that puts me at ease is to finish what I had started, my writing. Before, I would have been afraid to lay my dirty laundry out in public because I would have embarrassed my brother. Now we're both free, I love you Joe.

That's my story as of today and although I am not walking, my travels have been worth it just for the experiences of life and for the memories I have with Joe. As far as my paralysis, I feel that I have been at this job for eight years and for anyone that's been at a job for that long, you get good at it and don't even realize it. So when people tell me that I look good I don't even realize it because it's my job. My job is to "Go Forward" like my mentor Christopher Reeve.

Made in the USA
Columbia, SC
09 March 2022